COMRADELY GREETINGS

COMRADELY GREETINGS

The Prison Letters of Nadya and Slavoj

NADEZHDA TOLOKONNIKOVA
AND SLAVOJ ŽIŽEK

Translated by Ian Dreiblatt
Introduced by Michel Eltchaninoff

VERSO
London • New York

First published by Verso 2014
The collection © Verso 2014
Introduction translation © David Broder 2014
Nadya's letters translation © Ian Dreiblatt 2014
Slavoj's letters © Slavoj Žižek 2014
"The True Blasphemy" first published by *chtodelat news* 2012
© Slavoj Žižek 2012, 2014
"Why I Am Going on Hunger Strike" first published by *n+1* 2013
Translation © Bela Shayevich and Thomas Campbell 2013, 2014
Nadya's August 23 letter and Slavoj's August 26 letter first
published by mark-feygin.livejournal.com

1 3 5 7 9 10 8 6 4 2

Verso
UK: 6 Meard Street, London W1F 0EG
US: 20 Jay Street, Suite 1010, Brooklyn, NY 11201
www.versobooks.com

Verso is the imprint of New Left Books

ISBN-13: 978-1-78168-773-4 (PB)
eISBN-13: 978-1-78168-774-1 (US)
eISBN-13: 978-1-78168-775-8 (UK)

British Library Cataloguing in Publication Data
A catalogue record for this book is available from the British Library

Library of Congress Cataloging-in-Publication Data
A catalog record for this book is available from the Library of Congress

Typeset in Fournier by MJ & N Gavan, Truro, Cornwall
Printed in the US by Maple Press

Contents

Introduction

At around 11 a.m. on February 21, 2012, an event unheard of in contemporary Russia played out in the country's largest and most famous Orthodox church. The monumental Cathedral of Christ the Savior stands out in the skyline not far from the Kremlin, on the bank of the river Moskva. Constructed in the nineteenth century to commemorate the victory over Napoleon, the ultimate symbol of Tsarist power and seat of the Moscow Patriarchate, it was destroyed by the Soviet authorities and then rebuilt in the 1990s to mark the rebirth of Christianity in Russia after decades of official atheism. It was consecrated in 2000, at the very moment of Vladimir Putin's accession to the presidency. But for many intellectuals it is a place which equally symbolizes the ostentatious pomp of an ecclesiastical hierarchy sporting expensive watches and luxury cars, who support the Kremlin leadership without fail while providing it with an ideological basis founded on "traditional values" and the boundless exaltation of "Holy Russia." To launch an attack here is to hit at the very heart—metaphorical, but also very real—of contemporary Russian power.

There is no service, this particular Tuesday morning.
The immense space is very calm. Five young women pass
the security checks without hindrance. They rapidly head
over to the raised platform in front of the altar, reserved
for the reading of sacred texts by the clergy. They slip on
red, blue, orange, yellow, and violet balaclavas. They take
off their coats, revealing their brightly colored dresses and
tights. The female maintenance staff start to panic and call
security. One security guard hurries across, tackles a young
woman holding a guitar and pulls her away. He returns to
grab hold of a loudspeaker. Church employees attempt to
intercept the other four. But they have already begun their
twenty-verse "punk prayer," whose refrain is "Virgin
Mary, Mother of God, Banish Putin." Their song robustly
denounces the corruption of today's Russian Church, its
ultra-conservative ideology ("Don't upset His Saintship
ladies / Stick to making love and babies"), the KGB past of
Moscow's Patriarch Cyril and his unconditional support for
Vladimir Putin's repressive policies ("Patriarch Gundyaev
believes in Putin / Better believe in God, you vermin!").
The punks, kneeling and crossing themselves dramatically,
conclude with the plea: "Join our protest, Holy Virgin." The
whole performance lasts a few dozen seconds at most, before
the women file out of the church, accompanied by the ten
people who had come to film and assist them.

As the first photos and videos circulated and began to
spread around the world, three members of the group were
arrested, placed under provisional detention, and charged
with hooliganism (Article 213 of the penal code). Nadezhda
Tolokonnikova (born in 1989), Maria Alyokhina (born in

1988), and Yekaterina Samutsevich (born in 1982) each faced up to seven years in prison.

This was not their first provocation. The hooded female punk group had emerged out of a radical contemporary art collective set up a few years earlier, in 2007, under the name Voina (War), initiated by Oleg Vorotnikov and Natalia Sokol. Nadya Tolokonnikova and her husband Piotr Verzilov were also members. Vorotnikov, Sokol, Tolokonnikova and Verzilov were students at the philosophy faculty of the prestigious Moscow State University, and were joined in the collective by other young people from St. Petersburg. Inspired by the actions staged by Russian artists like Alexander Brener and Oleg Kulik, the group began to organize provocative performances in public places. In February 2008, several couples, including the then-pregnant Nadya and Piotr, were photographed having sex in a hall of the Moscow Biological Museum. In June 2010, a giant painted phallus appeared on a bridge facing the FSB building in St. Petersburg, to the astonishment of passers-by. Combining contemporary art with political action, the collective quickly became one of the spearheads of artistic opposition to the Putin regime. In 2011, a number of its members, including Nadya Tolokonnikova and Katya Samutsevich, formed Pussy Riot.

At the end of that same year, the situation became increasingly troubling for the Russian leadership. On September 26, 2011, Dmitry Medvedev—then president and nearing the end of his term—announced that he would be handing power back to Vladimir Putin. Having been president from 2000 to 2008, Putin had had to, in effect, "lend" his protégé the presidency for four years. He could now return as the head of the country for two six-year terms—until 2024. All Vladimir Putin now had to do was make sure he won the election. Parts of Russian society were shocked by these far-from-democratic shenanigans, and had little love for a regime that appears to be lasting longer than did that of Leonid Brezhnev. The anger exploded after December 4, 2011, following parliamentary elections that handed victory to the Kremlin-controlled United Russia Party as a result of massive, and crude, electoral fraud. Street demonstrations in the larger towns and cities rallied tens, even hundreds of thousands of people. There had been no equivalent protests since the era of Perestroika. Pussy Riot participated enthusiastically, taking all sorts of risks. On January 20, 2012, eight group members performed a song mocking candidate Putin in the middle of Red Square, facing the Kremlin, the sacred site of political power. On February 21 they broke new ground by targeting the absolute taboo: the Russian Church hierarchy's support for Kremlin policy.

This time, it was too much. Three young women were arrested. After a hard-fought presidential campaign, in the end Putin was elected on March 4, 2012. Now came the systematic, brutal retaliation against those who had led the protests of the preceding winter, under various different pretexts. On August 17, at the end of a trial packed with solidarity demonstrations, and the arrest of sympathizers, the three members of Pussy Riot were sentenced to two years in a penal colony for "vandalism" and "incitement to religious hatred." The prosecutor's argument hinged on the blasphemous aspect of their action, even though such a notion was at that time absent from the Russian penal code. They appealed. Katya was released on October 10, but Nadya and Masha were sent to separate penal colonies—the former to Mordovia, the traditional home of the Soviet Gulags, and the latter to the Perm region.

While they were still in provisional detention in Moscow, the independent Russian weekly the *New Times* published an interview with the prisoners. Nadya explained the essentially political aspect of her action, begged pardon of any believers whom she might have offended. She resolutely took to the philosophical terrain, quoting Socrates and Diogenes. She confessed: "I am currently reading an essay by Slavoj Žižek, 'Violence' ... What Žižek writes is very important to us. According to him, the fundamentalist believers of each different religion emerge on account of their lack of true faith, not because of deep faith. I would really love to meet Žižek!"

Struck by this declaration of philosophical love, I wrote at once to Slavoj Žižek and proposed that he come to Moscow to meet Nadya. She was then still in the capital, awaiting the result of the appeal hearing. My plan was to publish their discussion in *Philosophie Magazine*, and Žižek quickly replied: "YES, of course!" I requested the help of Zoya Svetova, the *New Times* journalist who had published the interview in which Nadya voiced her admiration for Žižek and had access to detainees on account of her status as a prison visitor. While we were waiting for authorization, however, Tolokonnikova was sent from the detention center where she had been held throughout the trial to camp PC-14 in Mordovia, thousands of miles from Moscow. It was unrealistic to imagine going there with Žižek: no one would ever have given him authorization to visit. So in December 2012 I proposed to Slavoj that he begin a correspondence with Nadya. He accepted enthusiastically, emailing me his first letter.

The exchange of letters took place as follows: We had Žižek's letters translated from English into Russian, then sent them to Zoya Svetova. The Federal Penitentiary Service has an internal electronic messaging system, but Zoya, thanks to her prison visitor status, was able to send the texts to Nadya via a special access code. After being read and verified by prison officials, the messages were forwarded to the prisoner. Nadya responded, writing by hand on special forms. Her letters were then transcribed for the messaging system by the prison administration and sent to the correspondent— who pays for the cost of this service. The responses were also clearly subjected to censorship at the hands of the penal colony. Once Zoya received them and transmitted them to us, all that was left to do was translate them into English and forward them to Slavoj.

As an inevitable consequence of these various filters, the rhythm of the correspondence was very slow. Aware that prison authorities were reading her letters, Nadya avoided detailing her daily life in prison. In any case, she preferred to remain—as did her interlocutor—on the intellectual terrain. The result of their correspondence is in the image of these two personalities. A disjointed mélange of poetry, rage, and fine neo-Marxist dialectics, evidencing their extraordinary temperaments. But beyond this exceptional human encounter between a ringleader of global contestation and a symbol of its persecution, something more profound emerged. At the beginning, the dialogue was in part an expression of mutual admiration: Žižek saw the adventures of Pussy Riot as a manifestation of the "World Spirit," just as Hegel had seen Napoleon's cavalcade conquering Europe as the incarnation of a more general historical lesson. In his view, the members of the group were challenging both Putin's authoritarianism *and* the "Stalinization" of contemporary capitalism. Tolokonnikova, after recounting that she had recently dreamt of the philosopher, responded with a Nietzschean rallying-cry: "We are the children of Dionysus," she proclaimed, those sowing chaos among the established order. She also explicitly situated herself in the lineage of the great Russian thinker Nikolai Berdyaev, apostle of a spiritual liberty for the contemporary age and of a renewal of the religious as a revolt against worldly law. Considering her detention the logical outcome of her action, she courageously concluded—we later learned the terrible conditions she was imprisoned and working in at the time she wrote these lines—"When the World Spirit touches you, don't think you can walk away unscathed."

In his reply, Žižek critiqued a purely Nietzschean vision of Pussy Riot's struggle. The collective, he argued, was participating in a wider emancipatory movement: "Not just to shake people out of their complacent inertia, but to change the very coordinates of social reality such that, when things return to normal, there will be a new, more satisfying 'Apollonian equilibrium.'" According to him, to hold to an ethical position in the face of contemporary capitalism is not at all sufficient. Indeed, "one can no longer play the game of subverting the Order from the position of its part-of-no-part, since the Order has already internalized its own permanent subversion. With the full deployment of 'late capitalism' it is 'normal' life itself which, in a way, becomes 'carnivalized,' with its constant reversals, crises, and reinventions." We cannot oppose one carnival by promoting another. It was on this point that the exchange really fired up between the two interlocutors. Nadya posed to Slavoj a purely Marxist objection, anchored in her real: the ludic immaterial capitalism of Western "creatives" could not exist without a backyard too often ignored by Marxists themselves, namely the vast zone of exploitation of the poor in authoritarian regimes like China ... or Russia. And so the debate was on.

It is exciting to read for many reasons. We discover that Nadya Tolokonnikova is not only a punk protestor, but a great intellectual. She seems to have perfect mastery of the reference points of contemporary thought—among them Deleuze and Guattari, Hardt and Negri, and Badiou. To this she adds references to Russian religious philosophy. Above all, she combines theoretical knowledge, a practical philosophy of revolt through contemporary art, and the terrifying reality of a penal colony where prisoners are forced to make clothes for the Russian market in slave conditions. The trying experience of the camp led her to reflect on contemporary Marxist analysis, which she judges almost colonial insofar as its fascination with the immaterial economy and carnivalesque Western creativity causes it to forget the real exploitation going on in the East. Upbraided by this young thinker, Slavoj Žižek had to try his utmost to be convincing. In his letter addressed to the soon-to-be-freed Nadya, he presents her with a worldwide tour of voluntary servitude. In this interchange, the two intellectuals grounded their thinking in reality more than ever, and in the process offered a fierce and piercing analysis of the workings of the world.

Nadya Tolokonnikova and Masha Alyokhina were freed on December 23, 2013, when Putin released them two months early in order to open his Winter Olympics in Sochi without apparent strife. But their struggle has only just begun. And so, too, the dialogue between Nadya and Slavoj.

Michel Eltchaninoff
Philosopher and deputy editor-in-chief
of *Philosophie Magazine*

The True Blasphemy:

On the Pussy Riot Sentencing

Pussy Riot members accused of blasphemy and hatred of religion? The answer is easy: the true blasphemy is the state accusation itself, formulating as a crime of religious hatred something which was clearly a political act of protest against the ruling clique. Recall Brecht's old quip from his Beggars' Opera: "What is the robbing of a bank compared to the founding of a new bank?" In 2008, Wall Street gave us the new version: what is the stealing of a couple of thousand of dollars, for which one goes to prison, compared to financial speculations that deprive tens of millions of their homes and savings, and are then rewarded by state help of sublime grandeur? Now, we got another version from Russia, from the power of the state: What is a modest Pussy Riot obscene provocation in a church compared to the accusation against Pussy Riot, this gigantic obscene provocation of the state apparatus which mocks any notion of decent law and order?

Was the act of Pussy Riot cynical? There are two kinds of cynicism: the bitter cynicism of the oppressed which unmasks the hypocrisy of those in power, and the cynicism of the oppressors themselves who openly violate their own proclaimed principles. The cynicism of Pussy Riot is of the first kind, while the cynicism of those in power—why not call their authoritarian brutality a Prick Riot—is of the much more ominous second kind.

Back in 1905, Leon Trotsky characterized tsarist Russia as "a vicious combination of the Asian knout and the European stock market." Does this designation not hold more and more also for the Russia of today? Does it not announce the rise of the new phase of capitalism, capitalism with Asian values (which, of course, has nothing to do with Asia and everything to do with the anti-democratic tendencies in today's global capitalism). If we understand cynicism as ruthless pragmatism of power which secretly laughs at its own principles, then Pussy Riot are anti-cynicism embodied. Their message is: IDEAS MATTER. They are conceptual artists in the noblest sense of the word: artists who embody an Idea. This is why they wear balaclavas: masks of de-individualization, of liberating anonymity. The message of their balaclavas is that it doesn't matter which of them got arrested—they're not individuals, they're an Idea. And this is why they are such a threat: it is easy to imprison individuals, but try to imprison an Idea!

The panic of those in power—displayed by their ridiculously excessive brutal reaction—is thus fully justified. The more brutally they act, the more important symbol Pussy Riot will become. Already now the result of the oppressive measures is that Pussy Riot are a household name literally all around the world.

It is the sacred duty of all of us to prevent that the courageous individuals who compose Pussy Riot will not pay in their flesh the price for their becoming a global symbol.

Slavoj Žižek
August 7, 2012

Why I Am Going on Hunger Strike:

An Open Letter

On Monday, September 23, I am declaring a hunger strike. This is an extreme method, but I am absolutely convinced it is my only recourse in the current situation.

The prison wardens refuse to hear me. But I will not back down from my demands. I will not remain silent, watching in resignation as my fellow prisoners collapse under slave-like conditions. I demand that human rights be observed at the prison. I demand that the law be obeyed in this Mordovian camp. I demand we be treated like human beings, not slaves.

It has been a year since I arrived at Penal Colony No. 14 [PC-14] in the Mordovian village of Partsa. As the women convicts say, "Those who haven't done time in Mordovia haven't done time at all." I had heard about the Mordovian prison camps while I was still being held at Pre-Trial Detention Center No. 6 in Moscow. They have the harshest conditions, the longest workdays, and the most flagrant lawlessness. Prisoners see their fellows off to Mordovia as if they were headed to the scaffold. Until the last, they keep hoping: "Maybe they won't send you to Mordovia after all? Maybe the danger will pass you by?" It didn't pass me by, and in the autumn of 2012, I arrived in the prison country on the banks of the Partsa River.

My first impression of Mordovia was the words uttered by the prison's deputy warden, Lieutenant Colonel Kupriyanov, who actually runs PC-14. "You should know that when it comes to politics, I am a Stalinist." Colonel Kulagin, the other warden (the prison is administered in tandem) called me in for a chat my first day here in order to force me to confess my guilt. "A misfortune has befallen you. Isn't that right? You've been sentenced to two years in prison. People usually change their views when bad things happen to them. If you want to be paroled as soon as possible, you have to confess your guilt. If you don't, you won't get parole." I told him right away I would work only the eight hours a day stipulated by the Labor Code. "The code is the code. What really matters is making your quota. If you don't, you work overtime. And we've broken stronger wills than yours here!" Colonel Kulagin replied.

My whole shift works sixteen to seventeen hours a day in the sewing workshop, from seven-thirty in the morning to twelve-thirty at night. At best, we get four hours of sleep a night. We have a day off once every month and a half. We work almost every Sunday. Prisoners "voluntarily" apply to work on weekends. In fact, there is nothing "voluntary" about it. These applications are written involuntarily on the orders of the wardens and under pressure from the inmates who help enforce their will.

No one dares to disobey (that is, not apply to go to the manufacturing zone on Sunday, meaning going to work until one in the morning). Once, a fifty-year-old woman asked to go back to the dorm zone at eight p.m. instead of twelve-thirty p.m. so she could go to bed at ten p.m. and get eight hours of sleep just once that week. She was not feeling well; she had high blood pressure. In response, a dorm unit meeting was called, where the woman was scolded, humiliated, insulted, and branded a parasite. "What, do you think you're the only one who wants more sleep? You need to work harder, you're strong as a horse!" When someone from the shift doesn't come to work on doctor's orders, they're bullied as well. "I sewed when I had a fever of forty Centigrade, and it was fine. Who did you think was going to pick up the slack for you?"

I was welcomed to my dorm unit by a convict finishing up a nine-year sentence. "The pigs are scared to put the squeeze on you themselves. They want to have the inmates do it." Conditions at the prison really are organized in such a way that the inmates in charge of the work shifts and dorm units are the ones tasked by the wardens with crushing the will of inmates, terrorizing them, and turning them into speechless slaves.

There is a widely implemented system of unofficial punishments for maintaining discipline and obedience. Prisoners are forced to "stay in the local until lights out,"[1] meaning they are forbidden to go into the barracks, whether

---

1 The "local" is a fenced-off passageway between two areas in the camp.

it is fall or winter. In the second unit, where the disabled and elderly live, there was a woman who ended up getting such bad frostbite after a day in the local that her fingers and one of her feet had to be amputated. The wardens can also "shut down sanitation" (forbid prisoners to wash up or go to the toilet) and "shut down the commissary and the tearoom" (forbid prisoners to eat their own food and drink beverages). It's both funny and frightening when a forty-year-old woman tells you, "So we're being punished today! I wonder whether we'll be punished tomorrow, too." She can't leave the sewing workshop to pee or take a piece of candy from her purse. It's forbidden.

Dreaming only of sleep and a sip of tea, the exhausted, harassed and dirty convict becomes obedient putty in the hands of the administration, which sees us solely as a free work force. So, in June 2013, my monthly wages came to twenty-nine rubles—twenty-nine rubles![2] Our shift sews one hundred and fifty police uniforms per day. Where does the money made from them go?

The prison has been allocated funding to buy completely new equipment a number of times. However, the administration has only had the sewing machines repainted, with the convicts doing the work. We sew on obsolete and worn-out machines. According to the Labor Code, when equipment does not comply with current industry standards, production quotas must be lowered vis-à-vis standard industry norms. But the quotas only increase, abruptly and suddenly. "If you let them see you can deliver one hundred uniforms,

---

2 Approximately sixty-seven euro cents.

they'll raise the minimum to one hundred and twenty!" say veteran machine operators. And you cannot fail to deliver, either, or else the whole unit will be punished, the entire shift. Punished, for instance, by everyone being forced to stand on the parade ground for hours. Without the right to go to the toilet. Without the right to take a sip of water.

Two weeks ago, the production quotas for all prison work shifts were arbitrarily increased by fifty units. If previously the minimum was one hundred uniforms a day, now it is one hundred and fifty. According to the Labor Code, workers must be notified of a change in the production quota no less than two months before it goes into effect. At PC-14, we just woke up one day to find we had a new quota because the idea happened to have popped into the heads of the wardens of our "sweatshop" (that's what the prisoners call the penal colony). The number of people in the work shift decreases (they are released or transferred), but the quota grows. As a result, those who remain have to work harder and harder. The mechanics say they don't have the parts to repair the machinery and will not be getting them. "There are no spare parts! When will they come? What, you don't live in Russia? How can you ask such questions?" During my first few months in the manufacturing zone, I nearly mastered the profession of mechanic, out of necessity and on my own. I would attack my machine, screwdriver in hand, desperate to fix it. Your hands are scratched and poked by needles, your blood is all over the table, but you keep on sewing. You are part of an assembly line, and you have to do your job alongside the experienced seamstresses. Meanwhile, the damned machine keeps breaking down. Because you're the newcomer and there is a lack of good equipment in the prison, you end up with the worst equipment, the most worthless machine on the line. And now it's broken down again, and once again you run off looking for the mechanic, who is impossible to find. You are yelled at and berated for slowing down production. There are no sewing classes at the prison, either. Newcomers are immediately plunked down in front of their machines and given their assignments.

"If you weren't Tolokonnikova, you would have had the shit kicked out of you a long time ago," say fellow prisoners with close ties to the wardens. It's true: other prisoners are beaten up. For not being able to keep up. They hit them in the kidneys, in the face. Convicts themselves deliver these beatings and not a single one of them happens without the approval and knowledge of the wardens. A year ago, before I came here, a Gypsy woman was beaten to death in the third unit. (The third unit is the "pressure cooker": prisoners whom the wardens want subjected to daily beatings are sent there.) She died in the infirmary at PC-14. The administration was able to cover up the fact she had been beaten to death: a stroke was listed as the official cause of death. In another block, new seamstresses who couldn't keep up were undressed and forced to sew naked. No one dares complain to the wardens, because all they will do is smile and send the prisoner back to the dorm unit, where the "snitch" will be beaten on the orders of those same wardens. For the prison warden, managed hazing is a convenient method for forcing convicts to totally obey their lawless regime.

A threatening, anxious atmosphere pervades the manufacturing zone. Eternally sleep-deprived, overwhelmed by the endless race to fulfill inhumanly large quotas, the convicts are always on the verge of breaking down, screaming at each other, fighting over the smallest things. Just recently, a young woman got stabbed in the head with a pair of scissors because she didn't turn in a pair of pants on time. Another tried to cut her own stomach open with a hacksaw. She was stopped from finishing the job.

Those who found themselves at PC-14 in 2010, the year of smoke and wildfires,[3] said that when the fire would approach the prison walls, convicts continued to go to the manufacturing zone and fulfill their quotas. Because of the smoke you couldn't see a person standing two meters in front of you, but, covering their faces in wet kerchiefs, they all went to work anyway. Because of the emergency conditions, prisoners weren't taken to the cafeteria for meals. Several women told me they were so horribly hungry they started keep diaries to document the horror of what was happening to them. When the fires were finally put out, prison security diligently rooted out these diaries during searches so that nothing would be leaked to the outside world.

Sanitary conditions at the prison are calculated to make the prisoner feel like a disempowered, filthy animal. Although there are hygiene rooms in the dorm units, a "general hygiene room" has been set up for corrective and punitive purposes. This room can accommodate five people, but all eight hundred prisoners are sent there to wash up. We must not wash ourselves in the hygiene rooms in our barracks: that would be too easy. There is always a stampede

---

3 In 2010 several hundred wildfires broke out across Russia.

in the "general hygiene room" as women with little tubs try and wash their "wet nurses" (as they are called in Mordovia) as fast as they can, clambering on top of each other. We are allowed to wash our hair once a week. However, even this bathing day gets cancelled. A pump will break or the plumbing will be stopped up. At times, my dorm unit has been unable to bathe for two or three weeks.

When the pipes are clogged, urine gushes out of the hygiene rooms and clumps of feces go flying. We've learned to unclog the pipes ourselves, but it doesn't last long: they soon get stopped up again. The prison does not have a plumber's snake for cleaning out the pipes. We get to do laundry once a week. The laundry is a small room with three faucets from which a thin trickle of cold water flows.

Convicts are always given stale bread, generously watered-down milk, exceptionally rancid millet and only rotten potatoes for the same corrective ends, apparently. This summer, sacks of slimy, black potato bulbs were brought to the prison in bulk. And they were fed to us.

One could endlessly discuss workplace and living condition violations at PC-14. However, my main grievance has to do with something else. It is that the prison administration prevents in the harshest possible way all complaints and petitions regarding conditions at PC-14 from leaving the prison. The wardens force people to remain silent, stooping to the lowest and cruelest methods to this end. All the other problems stem from this one: the increased work quotas, the sixteen-hour workday, and so on. The wardens feel they have impunity, and they boldly crack down on prisoners more and more. I couldn't understand why everyone kept silent until I found myself facing the mountain of obstacles that crashes down on the convict who decides to speak out. Complaints simply do not leave the prison. The only chance is to complain through a lawyer or relatives. The administration, petty and vengeful, will meanwhile use all the means at its disposal for pressuring the convict so she will understand that her complaints will not make anything better for anyone, but will only make things worse. Collective punishment is employed: you complain about the lack of hot water, and they turn it off altogether.

In May 2013, my lawyer Dmitry Dinze filed a complaint about the conditions at PC-14 with the prosecutor's office. The prison's deputy warden, Lieutenant Colonel Kupriyanov, instantly made conditions at the camp unbearable. There was search after search, a flood of disciplinary reports on all my acquaintances, the seizure of warm clothes, and threats of seizure of warm footwear. At work, they got revenge with complicated sewing assignments, increased quotas, and fabricated defects. The forewoman of the neighboring unit, Lieutenant Colonel Kupriyanov's right hand, openly incited prisoners to sabotage the items I was responsible for in the manufacturing zone so there would be an excuse to send me to solitary confinement for damaging "public property." She also ordered the convicts in her unit to provoke a fight with me.

It is possible to tolerate anything as long as it affects you alone. But the method of collective correction at the prison is something else. It means that your unit, or even the entire prison, has to endure your punishment along with you. The most vile thing of all is that this includes people you've come to care about. One of my friends was denied parole, which she had been working towards for seven years by diligently overfulfilling quotas in the manufacturing zone. She was reprimanded for drinking tea with me. Lieutenant Colonel Kupriyanov transferred her to another unit the same day. Another close acquaintance of mine, a very cultured woman, was thrown into the pressure-cooker unit for daily beatings because she had read and discussed with me a Justice Department document entitled "Internal Regulations at Correctional Facilities." Disciplinary reports were filed on everyone who talked to me. It hurt me that people I cared about were forced to suffer. Laughing, Lieutenant Colonel Kupriyanov said to me then, "You probably don't have any friends left!" He explained it was all happening because of Dinze's complaints.

Now I see I should have gone on hunger strike back in May, when I first found myself in this situation. However, seeing the tremendous pressure put on other convicts, I stopped the process of filing complaints against the prison.

Three weeks ago, on August 30, I asked Lieutenant Colonel Kupriyanov to grant the prisoners in my work shift eight hours of sleep. The idea was to decrease the workday from sixteen to twelve hours. "Fine, starting Monday, the shift can even work eight hours," he replied. I knew this was another trap because it is physically impossible to make our increased quota in eight hours. So the work shift would lag behind and face punishment. "If they find out you were the one behind this," the lieutenant colonel continued, "you definitely will never have it bad again, because there is no such thing as bad in the afterlife." Kupriyanov paused. "And finally, never make requests for everyone. Make requests only for yourself. I've been working in the prison camps for many years, and whenever someone has come to me to request something for other people, they have always gone straight from my office to solitary confinement. You're the first person this won't happen to."

Over the following weeks, life in my dorm unit and work shift was made intolerable. Convicts close to the wardens incited the unit to violence. "You've been punished by having tea and food, bathroom breaks, and smoking banned for a week. And now you're always going to be punished unless you start treating the newcomers, especially Tolokonnikova, differently. Treat them like the old-timers used to treat you back in the day. Did they beat you up? Of course they did. Did they rip your mouths? They did. Fuck them up. You won't be punished for it."

I was repeatedly provoked to get involved in conflicts and fights, but what is the point of fighting with people who have no will of their own, who are only acting at the behest of the wardens?

The Mordovian convicts are afraid of their own shadows. They are completely intimidated. If only the other day they were well disposed toward me and begging me to do something about the sixteen-hour workday, they are afraid even to speak to me after the administration has come down hard on me.

I made the wardens a proposal for resolving the conflict. I asked that they release me from the pressure artificially manufactured by them and enacted by the prisoners they control, and that they abolish slave labor at the prison by reducing the length of the workday and decreasing the quotas to bring them into compliance with the law. But in response the pressure has only intensified. Therefore, as of September 23, I declare a hunger strike and refuse to be involved in the slave labor at the prison until the administration complies with the law and treats women convicts not like cattle banished from the legal realm for the needs of the garment industry, but like human beings.

Nadya Tolokonnikova
September 23, 2013

The Prison Letters of
Nadya and Slavoj

"All of our activity is a quest for miracles"

Nadya to Slavoj, August 23, 2012

Dear Slavoj,

We received the news that you have been supporting us in every way—in theory and in practice. How terrific! The three of us have been incredulous at the birth of this miraculous movement for political liberation, and your support will mean its continuation. I love miracles and strive for them. All of our activity is a quest for miracles. The inmates are studying your essay "Violence."

Thanks for everything!

Good luck to all.

Nadya

"Ignore all who pity you as punk provocateurs"

Slavoj to Nadya, August 26, 2012

Dear Nadezhda, dear Maria, dear all of you!

I got your letters in Russian, which I can read (I learned Russian in high school!). Unfortunately, I cannot any longer write in Russian, so forgive me my English.

I cannot tell you how proud I am to be in contact with you. Your acts are well thought, and based on deep insights into how oppressive power works, how it has to rely on a hidden obscene agenda, violating its own rules. But more than that, you show all of us the way to combine these right insights with simple courage. Against all postmodern cynics, you demonstrate that ethical-political engagement is needed more than ever. So please ignore enemies and false friends who pity you as punk provocateurs who deserve mere clemency. You are not helpless victims calling for sympathy and mercy, you are fighters calling for solidarity in struggle. From my own past in Slovenia, I am well aware of how punk performances are much more effective than liberal-humanitarian protests. My dream is, when all this mess is over, to have a long talk with you about all these matters.

But I am well aware that we are fragile human beings at the mercy of forces of oppression, and this is why I am also filled with sad rage and fury—why can I not do more to help you? Please just let me know how I can be of ANY help and I will do it, be it political or personal. Next week I go to Toronto to present the new film *The Pervert's Guide to Ideology*, and I will dedicate it to you.

It may sound crazy, but although I am an atheist, you are in my prayers. Prayers that you will soon see your family, children, friends. Prayers that you will at least have some time to read and reflect in peace while in prison!

All my love,

Slavoj

"It is so important that you persist"

Slavoj to Nadya, January 2, 2013

Dear Nadezhda,

I sincerely hope that you've been able to organize your life in prison around small rituals to make your stay there at least tolerable, and that you have some time to read. Here are my thoughts on your predicament.

John Jay Chapman, an American political essayist, wrote back in 1900 about radicals: "They are really always saying the same thing. They do not change; everybody else changes. They are accused of the most incompatible crimes, of egoism and a mania for power, indifference to the fate of their own cause, fanaticism, triviality, want of humor, buffoonery and irreverence. But they sound a certain note. Hence the great practical power of consistent radicals. To all appearance nobody follows them, yet everyone believes them. They hold a tuning-fork and sound A, and everybody knows it really is A, though the time-honored pitch is G flat." Is this not a fair description of the effect of a Pussy Riot performance? In spite of all the accusations, you sound a certain note. It may appear as if nobody is following you, but secretly they all believe you, they know you are telling the truth—or, even more so, that you stand for the truth.

But what truth? Why are the reactions to Pussy Riot performances so violent—and not only in Russia? The vacillations of the Western media are indicative here: all hearts were beating for you as long as you were seen as just another liberal-democratic protest against the authoritarian state; but the moment it became clear that you also reject global capitalism, the reports became much more ambiguous, with many now displaying a new-found "understanding" for your critics. Again, why?

What makes Pussy Riot so disturbing for the liberal gaze is the way you reveal a hidden continuity between Stalinism and contemporary global capitalism.

In one of his last interviews before his fall, Nicolae Ceaușescu was asked by a Western journalist why Romanian citizens were not free to travel abroad even though freedom of movement was guaranteed by the constitution. True, Ceaușescu replied, the constitution guarantees freedom of movement, but it also guarantees the right of the people to a safe homeland. So here we have a potential conflict of rights: if citizens were to be allowed to leave the country, the prosperity of Romania would be threatened and they would have endangered their right to a safe homeland. In such a conflict of rights then, one has to make a choice, and here the right to a prosperous and safe homeland enjoys the clear priority...

This same spirit of Stalinist sophistry remains alive and well in my own country, Slovenia, where on December 19, 2012, the Constitutional Court ruled that a proposed referendum on legislation to set up a "bad bank" would be unconstitutional, thus in effect banning any popular vote on the matter. The idea of the legislation was to transfer the bad debts of the major banks onto a new "bad bank" which would then be salvaged with state money (i.e., at the taxpayers' expense), preventing any serious inquiry into who was responsible for the debts. The measure had been debated for months and was far from being generally accepted even by financial specialists.

The popular vote on the issue had been proposed by trade unions opposed to the government's neoliberal economic policies, and their proposal had received enough signatures to make it obligatory. In the judgment of the Slovene Constitutional Court, however, such a referendum "would have caused unconstitutional consequences"—how? The Court conceded that a referendum was a constitutional right, but claimed that its execution in this case would endanger other constitutional values which, in a situation of deep economic crisis, should take priority—values such as the efficient functioning of the state apparatus, especially in creating the conditions for economic growth; or the realization of human rights, especially the rights to social security and to free economic activity... In short, in its assessment,

the Court simply accepted as undisputed fact the rea-
soning of the international financial authorities exerting
pressure on Slovenia to pursue more austerity measures. A
failure to obey the dictates of those authorities, or to meet
their expectations, the Court argued, would lead to further
political and economic crises and would thus be unconstitutional—in other words, since following those dictates is a
condition for the maintenance of constitutional order, they
take priority over the constitution (and *eo ipso* over state
sovereignty).

Slovenia may be a small marginal country, but this decision of its Constitutional Court is symptomatic of a global
tendency towards the limitation of democracy. The idea is
that, in a complex economic situation such as we have today,
the majority of people are not qualified to judge—they just
want to keep their privileges intact, and are ignorant of
the catastrophic consequences which would ensue if their
demands were to be met. This line of argumentation is not
new. In a TV interview a few years ago, Ralf Dahrendorf
linked the growing distrust in democracy to the fact that,
after every revolutionary change, the road to new prosperity will lead through a "valley of tears": with the breakdown
of socialism we cannot pass directly to the abundance of a
market economy—the limited, but real, socialist welfare
and security systems will first have to be dismantled, and
these initial steps will inevitably be painful. For Dahrendorf,
the key problem is that this passage through the "valley of
tears" will invariably last longer than the average period
between democratic elections, thereby creating an irre-
sistible temptation to postpone the difficult changes for

short-term electoral gain. But if the majority are likely to resist the necessary restructuring, would the logical conclusion not then be that, for a decade or so, an enlightened elite should take power, even by non-democratic means, in order to enforce the necessary measures and thus lay the foundations for a truly stable democracy? When developing countries are "prematurely democratized," the result is a populism which ends in economic catastrophe and political despotism—no wonder then that today's most economically successful Third World countries (Taiwan, South Korea, Chile) embraced full democracy only after a period of authoritarian rule. Does this line of thinking not also provide the best justification for the maintenance of an authoritarian regime in China?

What is new today is that, with the continuation of the crisis that began in 2008, this same distrust of democracy, once limited to Third World or post-Communist countries, is gaining ground in the developed Western countries themselves. What, a decade or two ago, was merely patronizing advice to others, now concerns ourselves, as Western Europe, in its passage from the post-war Welfare State to the new global economy, is required to undergo a painful restructuring leading to widespread insecurity.

But what if this distrust is justified? What if it is only the experts who can save us, whether with full or less than full democracy? The least one can say is that since 2008 the crisis has furnished us with more than adequate proof of how it is not the people but the experts themselves who, in the vast majority, have no idea what they are doing. In Western Europe, we are effectively witnessing the increasing inability of the ruling elite to rule. Look at how they've dealt with the Greek crisis: putting pressure on Greece to repay its debts while at the same time ruining its economy through imposed austerity measures—thereby ensuring that the debts will never be repaid.

No wonder, then, that Pussy Riot makes us all uneasy—you know very well what you don't know, you don't pretend to have fast and easy answers, but what you are also telling us is that those in power don't know either. Your message is that, in Europe today, the blind are leading the blind. This is why it is so important that you persist. In the same way that, after witnessing Napoleon entering Jena, Hegel wrote that it was as if he had seen the World Spirit riding in on a horse, you, sitting there in prison, embody nothing less than the critical awareness of us all.

Comradely greetings,

Slavoj

"We count ourselves among those rebels who court storms"

Nadja to Slavoj, February 23, 2013

Dear Slavoj,

One time, in the autumn of 2012, while I was sitting in pre-trial detention with the other Pussy Riot activists, I came to your house for a visit. In a dream, of course.

I get what you're saying about horses and the World Spirit, about Chapman's "buffoonery and irreverence," and more to the point about how and why all of these are so forcefully bound up with one another. Pussy Riot has wound up on the side of those who feel the call to critique, to creation and co-creation, to experimentation and the role of the unceasing provocateur. To put it in terms of the opposition

Nietzsche set up, we're the children of Dionysus, floating by in a barrel, accepting nobody's authority. We're on the side of those who don't offer final answers or transcendent truths. Our mission, rather, is the asking of questions.

There are architects of Apollonian equilibrium in this world, and there are (punk) singers of flux and transformation. One is not better than the other: "Mamy raznye nuzhny, mamy raznye vazhny."[1] Only our cooperation can ensure the continuity of Heraclitus' vision: "This world has always been and will always be a pulsing fire, flaring up accordingly, and dying down accordingly, with the cycling of the eternal world breath."

We count ourselves among those rebels who court storms,[2] who hold that the only truth lies in perpetual seeking.

Nikolai Berdyaev wrote in *Self-Knowledge*: "Truth as an object which intrudes itself and wields authority over me—an object in the name of which it is demanded that I should renounce freedom—is a figment: truth is no extraneous thing; it is the way and the life. Truth is spiritual conquest; it is known in and through freedom." "Christianity itself is to me the embodiment of the revolt against the world and its laws and fashions." "From time to time a terrible thought

---

1   A line from the popular Soviet children's writer Sergei Mikhalkov: "Moms of all kinds are needed, and moms of all kinds are important."

2   Tolokonnikova here is quoting from Mikhail Lermontov's 1832 poem "The Sail," a classic many Russians can recite from memory. The poem ends: "[The sail,] rebellious, courts a storm, / As though in storms it might find peace!"

crossed my mind: what if obsequious orthodoxy is right and I am wrong? In that case I am lost. But I have always been quick to cast this thought from me." All statements that might have come from Pussy Riot just as easily as from Russia's great political philosopher. In 1898, Berdyaev was arrested on charges of agitating for the Social Democrats, indicted for "designs on the overthrow of the government and the church," and exiled from Kiev for three years to the Vologda Gubernia. When the World Spirit touches you, don't think you can walk away unscathed.

◆

Intuition—and this is where your blind leading the blind comes in—is of stunning importance. The main thing is to realize that you yourself are as blind as can be. Once you get that, you can, for maybe the first time, doubt the natural place in the world to which your skin and your bones have rooted you, the inherited condition that constantly threatens to spill over into feelings of terror.

It's tempting to think that fundamentalism is the only terrifying aspect of our situation, but the problem is bigger than that; fundamentalists are the tip of the iceberg. There's a powerful antifascist dictum that "the fascists do the killing, the authorities the burying." I remember something the curator Andrei Erofeev,[3] whom I know to be anything but

---

3 In 2010, Erofeev and his colleague Yuri Samodurov were tried and convicted on the charge of "inciting religious hatred." Members of the artists' collective Voina (War) stormed into the courtroom during sentencing, with the intention of releasing several thousand live cockroaches. Among those involved in the action was Yekaterina

indifferent to antifascism, used to say while he was on trial at the instigation of the ultra-conservative People's Council, and facing considerable jail time, for his role in organizing the "Forbidden Art—2006" exhibition: "If the People's Council had acted without the sanction of state apparatuses, this trial wouldn't be happening. So the situation, fraught as it is with the crescendoing possibility of violence, is reproduced by those same 'experts' who, from where they stand in the halls of power, are supposed to be able to make impartial decisions. 'Only an expert can deal with the problem.'"

◆

That's something Laurie Anderson sings: "Only an expert can deal with the problem." If only Laurie and I could've had the chance to take those experts down a peg! And solve our problems without them. Because expert status is no portal to the Kingdom of Absolute Truth.

Reasonable minds at last are seeing how truth can come from the mouths of innocents. It's not in vain that the Rus'[4] so esteems its holy fools, its mad ones. In the beating, political heart of civil Russia's capital city, at the site of Pussy Riot's January 2012 performance, at the base of Red Square, stands St. Basil's Cathedral, named after Russia's beloved Basil Fool for Christ.

Cultural competence and sensitivity to the zeitgeist don't come with a college diploma or live in an administrator's

Samutsevich, who would later be arrested for participating in Pussy Riot's "Punk Prayer" alongside Tolokonnikova and Alyokhina.

4   An antiquated name for the earliest Slavic polities in the area of contemporary Russia; roughly akin to calling England "Britannia."

briefcase. You need to know which way to point the map. "Humor, buffoonery, and irreverence" might turn out to be modes of seeking truth. Truth is multifaceted, its seekers many and varied. "Different but equal," as another good antifascist slogan had it.

◆

I think Plato was pretty much wrong when he defined human beings as "featherless bipeds." No, a person does a lot more doubting than a plucked cock does. And these are the people I love—the Dionysians, the unmediated ones, those drawn to what's different and new, seeking movement and inspiration over dogmas and immutable statutes. The innocents, in other words, the speakers of truth.

Two years for Pussy Riot—the price we owe fate for the gift of perfect pitch that enables us to sound out an A, even while our old traditions teach us to listen for G-flat.

◆

How can we resolve the opposition between experts and innocents? I don't know. But this I can tell you: the party of the innocents, as in Herod's time, will exemplify resistance. We'll find our own basket and Pharaoh's daughter to help us. Those who keep a childlike faith in the triumph of truths over lies, and in mutual aid, who live their lives entirely within the gift economy, will always receive a miracle at the exact moment they need it.

Nadya
PC-14, Mordovia

"Is our position utopian?"

Slavoj to Nadya, April 4, 2013

Dear Nadya,

I was so pleasantly surprised by the arrival of your letter—the long delay had raised a fear in me that the authorities will prevent our communication.

I was deeply honored, flattered even, by my appearance in your dream. For me, appearing in a dream is forever associated with a precise date—the night of June 25, 1935, when Trotsky in exile dreamt that the dead Lenin was questioning him anxiously about his illness: "I answered that I already had many consultations and began to tell him about my trip to Berlin; but looking at Lenin I recalled that he was dead. I immediately tried to drive away this thought, so as to finish the conversation. When I had finished telling him about my therapeutic trip to Berlin in 1926, I wanted to add, 'This was after your death'; but I checked myself and said, 'After you fell ill …' "

There is an obvious link with the Freudian dream in which a father who doesn't know that he's dead appears to the dreamer. So what does it mean that Lenin doesn't know he's dead? There are two radically opposed ways of reading Trotsky's dream. According to the first, the terrifyingly ridiculous figure of the undead Lenin who doesn't know that he's dead stands for our own obstinate refusal to renounce our grandiose utopian projects and accept the limitations of our situation: there is no big Other, Lenin was mortal and made errors like everyone else, so it is time for us to let him die, put to rest this obscene ghost haunting our political imaginary, and approach our problems in a pragmatic, non-ideological way. But there is another sense in which Lenin is still alive: he is alive insofar as he embodies what Alain Badiou calls the "eternal Idea" of universal emancipation, the immortal striving for justice that no insult or catastrophe will manage to kill—Lenin lives wherever there are people who still fight for the same Idea.

Is this not our predicament today? And by "our" I mean those who remain faithful to the radical emancipatory (in short, Communist) political vision. Are we to be dismissed as dangerous utopians harboring new catastrophes, or— to quote your wonderful concluding thought—will there always be a miracle at the right moment in the lives of those with a childlike faith in the triumph of truths over lies? We should not be ashamed to evoke here, as you do, the tradition of the "fools for Christ." Is our position utopian? I am more and more convinced that today's real utopians are those pragmatic-rational experts who seem to believe that the present state of things can go on indefinitely, that we are not approaching the moment of an apocalyptic choice. If nothing in fact changes, then all of a sudden we will find ourselves living in a much darker society.

You are right to question the idea that "Only the experts can solve our problems." Maybe there are certain kinds of problems they can solve, but what they cannot do is to identify and formulate the true problems. Experts are by definition the servants of those in power: they don't really THINK, they just apply their knowledge to problems defined by the powerful (How to restore stability? How to crush the protest?, etc.). So when, dear Nadya, you ask: "How can we resolve the opposition between experts and innocents?", my first answer is that, in a way, it has already been resolved by contemporary global capitalism. That is to say, are today's capitalists, especially the so-called financial wizards, really the experts they claim to be? Or are they not rather stupid babies playing with our money and our fate?

Here I can't help but recall a cruel joke from Ernst Lubitsch's *To Be Or Not to Be*: when the Nazi commanding officer nicknamed "Concentration Camp Ehrhardt" is asked about the camps in occupied Poland, he snaps back: "We do the concentrating, the Poles do the camping." Something similar holds for the Enron bankruptcy back in January 2001, which can be interpreted as a kind of ironic commentary on the notion of the risk society, and indeed on the much greater financial catastrophes that were to follow. The thousands of employees who lost their jobs and savings were certainly exposed to risk, but without having had any real choice in the matter—the risk appeared to them like blind fate. Those who, on the contrary, did have a genuine knowledge of the risks involved—as well as the power to intervene in the situation—minimized their exposure by cashing in their stocks and options before the bankruptcy. While it is true, then, that we live in a society of risky choices, it is one in which only some (the Wall Street managers) do the choosing, while others (the people with mortgages) do the risking…

But I would like to raise some questions with regard to your Nietzschean notion of the power of truth and creativity embodied in "the children of Dionysus, floating by in a barrel, accepting nobody's authority." You rely here on Nietzsche's couple of the Apollonian and the Dionysian: "there are architects of Apollonian equilibrium in this world, and there are (punk) singers of flux and transformation. One is not better than the other … Only their cooperation can ensure the continuity of the world." Here, I must admit, I see some problems.

First, is it enough to just oppose the two principles and then postulate the need for some kind of balance between them? The least one can add is that there are different kinds of "Apollonian stasis"—Stalinist, fascist, capitalist, etc. For me, the true and most difficult task of radical emancipatory movements is not just to shake people out of their complacent inertia, but to change the very coordinates of social reality such that, when things return to normal, there will be a new, more satisfying "Apollonian equilibrium." How does contemporary global capitalism fit into this scheme? The Deleuzian philosopher Brian Massumi clearly formulated how today's capitalism has already overcome the logic of totalizing normality and adopts instead a logic of erratic excess: the more varied, and even erratic, the better. Normalcy starts to lose its hold. The regularities start to loosen. This loosening of normalcy is part of capitalism's dynamic. It's not a simple liberation. It's capitalism's own form of power. It's no longer disciplinary institutional power that defines everything, it's capitalism's power to produce variety—because markets get saturated. Produce variety and you produce a niche market. The oddest of affective tendencies are okay—as long as they pay. Capitalism starts intensifying or diversifying affect, but only in order to extract surplus-value. It hijacks affect in order to intensify profit potential. It literally valorizes affect. The capitalist logic of surplus-value production starts to take over the relational field that is also the domain of political ecology, the ethical field of resistance to identity and predictable paths. It's very troubling and confusing, because it seems to me that there's been a certain kind of convergence between the dynamic of capitalist power and the dynamic of resistance.

One can supplement this analysis in many directions. For instance, the very process of creating "liberated territories" outside the domain of State has itself been reappropriated by capitalism. Exemplary here are the so-called "Special Economic Zones": geographical regions within a (usually) Third World state enjoying more liberal economic laws designed to attract greater foreign investment—low or zero taxes, free flow of capital, limitation or prohibition of trade unions, no minimum wage requirement, etc. The SEZ label covers a whole range of more specific zone types such as Free Trade Zones, Export Processing Zones, Free Zones,

Industrial Estates, Free Ports, Urban Enterprise Zones, etc. With their unique combination of "openness" (as free spaces partially exempt from state sovereignty) and closure (discipline unencumbered by legally guaranteed freedoms), which renders possible the heightened exploitation, these Zones are the structural counterparts of the celebrated communities of "intellectual labor"; they are the fourth term in the tetrad of high-tech intellectual labor, gated communities, and slums.

What happens then, when the system no longer excludes the excess, but directly posits it as its driving force—as is the case when capitalism can only reproduce itself through a continual self-revolutionizing, a constant overcoming of its own limits? Then one can no longer play the game of subverting the Order from the position of its part-of-no-part, since the Order has already internalized its own permanent subversion. With the full deployment of "late capitalism" it is "normal" life itself which, in a way, becomes "carnivalized," with its constant reversals, crises, and reinventions, such that it is now the critique of capitalism, from a "stable" ethical position, which increasingly appears as the exception. Of course, the egalitarian-emancipatory "deterritorialization" is not the same as the postmodern-capitalist one, but the latter nonetheless radically changes the terms of the struggle insofar as the enemy is no longer the established hierarchic order of a State. How, then, are we to revolutionize an order whose very principle is one of a constant self-revolutionizing?

More than a solution to the problems we are facing today, Communism is itself the name of a problem: of the difficult task of breaking out of the confines of the market-and-state framework, a task for which no quick formula is at hand: "It's just the simple thing that's hard, so hard to do," as Brecht put it in his "In Praise of Communism."

The key here is to maintain a proper sense of orientation, and it's here that I totally agree with your profound insight that the fundamentalists are merely "the tip of the iceberg. There's a powerful antifascist dictum that 'the fascists do the killing, the authorities the burying.'" This is the crucial point always to bear in mind when those in power try to deflect our critical energies towards different forms of (religious, nationalist…) fundamentalism: from the Tea Party in the US to the West Bank settlers in Israel and the Orthodox nationalists in Russia, "fundamentalists" are, for all their apparent passion, ultimately puppets used and manipulated by the cold logic of state power. The task is not to crush them, but to try to redirect their passion against those who use and manipulate them. Did you notice how the religious fundamentalists in the US took over the very form of Leftist popular protest (grassroots self-organization against State power) and redirected it against the Leftist tradition?

But, my dear Nadya, I feel a certain sense of guilt in writing these lines: who am I to explode in such narcissistic theoretical outbursts when you, as a concrete individual, are exposed to very real empirical deprivations. So please, if you can and want to, do let me know about your situation in the prison: about the daily rhythm, about (maybe) the small private rituals which make it easier to survive, about how much time you have to read and write, about how the other prisoners (and the guards) treat you, about your contacts with your child … I have always thought that true heroism

lies in these apparently small ways of organizing one's life
so as to survive in crazy times without losing one's dignity.

  With all my love, respect, and admiration, my thoughts
are with you!

Slavoj

"I write you from a Special Economic Zone"

Nadya to Slavoj, April 16, 2013

Dear Slavoj,

You really think "today's capitalism has already overcome the logic of totalizing normality"? I say maybe it hasn't—maybe it just really wants us to *believe* it has, to accept that hierarchization and normalization have been exceeded.

You mention places where the legal rights that limit exploitation are suspended in the name of the world capitalist order. At this very moment, I write you from a Special Economic Zone. Seeing it with my eyes, feeling it on my skin.

As a kid I wanted to work in advertising. I had a whole romance with it. So now I know how to evaluate advertisements and commercials. I get the finer points. I even appreciate the things that by definition they have to keep silent about.

Late capitalism's anti-hierarchic and rhizomatic posture amounts to good advertising. You and Brian Massumi are right to point out that capitalism today has to *appear* loose, even erratic. That's how it captures affect—the affect of the consumer. When it comes to manufacturers (especially the ones who aren't located in high-tech business parks) this 'velvet' capitalism can afford to change its stripes. But the logic of totalizing normality still has to continue its work in those places whose industrial bases are used to shore up everything dynamic, adaptable, and incipient in late capitalism. And here, in this other world hidden from view, the governing logic is one of absolutely rigid standards, of stability reinforced with steel. Erratic behavior is not tolerated from workers here; homogeneity and stagnation rule. No wonder authoritarian China has emerged as a world economic leader.

Modern capitalism has a deep interest in seeing that you and I believe the system runs completely on principles of free creativity, limitless growth, and diversity, and that the flip side—millions of people enslaved by all-powerful and (take it from me) fantastically stable standards of production—remains invisible. We have an interest in exposing this deception, which is why I insist on unmasking the static, centralized, hierarchic basis of what advertising will later sanctify as a product of unbridled creativity alone.

That's why I take exception to your distrust of thinking that is posited within the frameworks of binary oppositions, and even insist on the use of such binaries as a heuristic—one that is situational and, when it must be, even burlesque. This is exactly how I deploy the opposition between Apollonian equilibrium and Dionysian flux. And given the broad expansion of fundamentalist tendencies in politics and economics, I'm sure we can't yet write off the suggestion of militant workers that economic growth and ecological conservation must be antithetical.

◆

With regard to the techniques that the global economy's intellectual and ad-industry core has developed for escaping static identities of subjugation, my feeling is that we need to find a way of joining this game without checking our beliefs at the door. We can definitely profit from the ping-pong being played between an egalitarian-emancipatory "deter-ritorialization" and the postmodern, capitalist one. But we have to stay brave, energetic, and stubborn—we can't walk away from the fight. Sparring is how you build endurance, how you learn to be quick on your feet and develop a sense of humor. Unlike the old Left, we can't just reject capitalism out of hand—we'll get further by playing with it, teasing till it's been perverted. Perverted, I mean, in the sense of being turned to face us, enlisted into our cause.

◆

Don't waste your time worrying about giving in to theoretical fabrications while I supposedly suffer "empirical deprivations." There's value to me in these inviolable limits, in my being tested this way. I'm fascinated to see how I'll cope with all this, how I'll channel it into something productive for my comrades and myself. I'm finding inspiration in here, ways of evolving. Not because but in spite of the system. Your thoughts and anecdotes are a help to me as I negotiate this conundrum. I'm glad we're in touch.

I await your reply.

Wishing you luck in our common cause,

Nadya

"Beneath the dynamics of your acts, there is inner stability"

Slavoj to Nadya, June 10, 2013

Dear Nadya,

Let me begin by confessing that I felt deeply ashamed after reading your reply. You wrote: "Don't waste your time worrying about giving in to theoretical fabrications while I supposedly suffer 'empirical deprivations.'" This simple sentence made me aware of the falsity of the final turn in my last letter: my expression of sympathy with your plight basically meant, "I have the privilege of doing real theory and teaching you about it while you are basically good for reporting on your experiences of hardship"... Your last letter abundantly demonstrates that you are much more than that, that you are an equal partner in a theoretical dialogue. So my sincere apologies for this proof of how deeply entrenched male chauvinism can be, especially when it is masked as sympathy for the other's suffering, and let me go on with our dialogue.

First just a minor remark. I deeply appreciate your point about the advertising industry—I am myself so tired of the purist pseudo-Marxist critique of advertising as part of commodity fetishism that I am almost tempted to propose the following guideline: a critical social theorist who is not able to enjoy advertisements should not be taken seriously… But let me now pass to our key *differend*. (Sorry that I use so many quotes—but others have formulated things much better than I am able to.) Your central point is that the anti-hierarchical structures and rhizomes of late capitalism are a deceiving facade that conceals hierarchical structures and normalization: beneath all the glitz of free creativity there is the same old static, centralized, and hierarchic material production base. With this I fully agree … up to a point. I, of course, agree that beneath the much-celebrated postmodern dynamics of global capitalism lie deeply entrenched structures of domination and exploitation. But are these structures of domination and exploitation still "the same old static, centralized, and hierarchic material production base"? Permit me to quote here a well-known passage from *The Communist Manifesto* which is valid today more than ever:

> The bourgeoisie cannot exist without constantly revolutionizing the instruments of production, and thereby the relations of production, and with them the whole relations

of society. Conservation of the old modes of production in
unaltered form was, on the contrary, the first condition of
existence for all earlier industrial classes. Constant revolutionizing of production, uninterrupted disturbance of
all social conditions, everlasting uncertainty and agitation
distinguish the bourgeois epoch from all earlier ones. All
fixed, fast-frozen relations, with their train of ancient and
venerable prejudices and opinions are swept away, all new-
formed ones become antiquated before they can ossify. All
that is solid melts into air, all that is holy is profaned.

It is this crazy dynamic of global capitalism that makes
effective resistance to it so difficult and frustrating. The rage
exploding across Europe today is, as Franco Berardi put it
in *After the Future*, "impotent and inconsequential, as con-
sciousness and coordinated action seem beyond the reach
of present society. Look at the European crisis. Never in
our life have we faced a situation so charged with revolutionary opportunities. Never in our life have we been so
impotent. Never have intellectuals and militants been so
silent, so unable to find a way to show a new possible direc-
tion." Berardi locates the origin of this impotence in the
explosive speed of the functioning of the big Other (the
symbolic substance of our lives) and the slowness of human
reactivity (due to culture, corporeality, diseases, etc.): "the
long-lasting neoliberal rule has eroded the cultural bases of
social civilization, which was the progressive core of modernity. And this is irreversible. We have to face it." Recall the
great wave of protests that spread all over Europe in 2011,
from Greece and Spain to London and Paris. Even if for the

most part there was no consistent political program mobilizing the protesters, their protests did function as part of a large-scale educational process: the protesters' misery and discontent were transformed into a great collective act of mobilization—hundreds of thousands gathered in public squares, proclaiming that they had enough, that things cannot go on like this. However, such protests, although they constitute the individuals participating in them as universal political subjects, remain at the level of a purely formal universality: what they stage is a purely negative gesture of angry rejection and an equally abstract demand for justice, lacking the ability to translate this demand into a concrete political program. In short, these protests were not yet proper political acts, but abstract demands addressed to an Other who is expected to act ...

One cannot but note the cruel irony of this contrast between Berardi and Hardt/Negri. Hardt and Negri celebrate "cognitive capitalism" as opening up a path towards "absolute democracy," since the object, the "stuff," of immaterial work is increasingly social relations themselves. Their wager is that this directly socialized, immaterial production not only renders owners progressively superfluous (who needs them when production is directly social, formally and in terms of its content?), but the producers also master the regulation of social space, since social relations (politics) *is* the stuff of their work: economic production directly becomes political production, the production of society itself. Berardi's conclusion is the exact opposite: far from bringing out the potential transparency of social life, today's "cognitive capitalism" makes it more impenetrable than ever, undermining the very conditions of any form of collective solidarity among the "cognitariat." What is symptomatic here is the way the same conceptual apparatus leads to two radically opposed conclusions.

If we are not able to step outside the compulsion of the system, the gap between the frantic dynamics it imposes and our corporeal and cognitive limitations sooner or later brings about a fall into depression. Berardi makes this point apropos his friend Félix Guattari, who, in theory, preached a gospel of hyper-dynamic "de-territorialization," while personally suffering from long bouts of depression:

> Actually the problem of depression and of exhaustion is never elaborated in an explicit way by Guattari. I see here a crucial problem of the theory of desire: the denial of the problem of limits in the organic sphere … The notion of the "body without organs" hints at the idea that the organism isn't something that you can define, that the organism is a process of exceeding, of going beyond a threshold, of "becoming other." This is a crucial point, but it's also a dangerous point … What body, what mind is going through transformation and becoming? Which invariant lies under the process of becoming other? If you want to answer this question you have to acknowledge death, finitude, and depression.

What can be done in a situation where demonstrations and protests prove to be of no use, where democratic elections fail to make any difference? According to Berardi, only withdrawal, passivity, and the abandonment of illusions can open up a new way: "Only self-reliant communities leaving the field of social competition can open a way to a new hope." I, of course, do not follow him here, but I do share his skepticism about chaotic resistance. I am more and more convinced that what really matters is what happens the day after: can we convince the tired and manipulated crowds that we are not only ready to undermine the existing order, to engage in provocative acts of resistance, but are also able to offer the prospect of a new order?

I think that Pussy Riot's performances cannot be reduced to being just subversive provocations. Beneath the dynamics of your acts, there is the inner stability of a firm ethico-political attitude. Pussy Riot does not propose merely a Dionysian destabilization of the existing static order—in a deeper sense, it is today's society that is caught in a crazy capitalist dynamic with no inner sense or measure, and it is Pussy Riot which de facto offers a stable ethico-political point. Pussy Riot's very existence communicates to thousands the fact that opportunist cynicism is not the only option, that we are not totally disoriented, that there still is a common cause worth fighting for.

So what I wish you is also good luck in our common cause. To be faithful to that cause means to be brave, especially today—and, as the old saying goes, fortune favors the brave!

Yours,

Slavoj

"As I serve my 'deuce'
in lockdown"

Nadya to Slavoj, July 13, 2013

Dear Slavoj,

Let me start this letter out by drawing a distinction I find crucial to avoiding the pitfalls of fictive universalization.

At the beginning of your letter, you caught yourself in a moment of male chauvinism. But I'm inclined to think you and I and our whole conversation are susceptible to a more justified—and so heavier—charge: that of a colonial perspective. What I mean is that we haven't so far been accounting for regional differences and quirks in the operation of the economic and political mechanisms we're discussing. This omission, this silence, feels suddenly shameful. Seduced by your arguments, I fell unreflectingly into the classic trap of exclusive and discriminatory universalization. And in the end, like anyone toying with unfounded universals, I excluded and discriminated against myself.

The difference I feel a civic duty to stipulate is between how what you call "global capitalism" works in the US or Europe, and how that same capitalism works in Russia. From where I'm sitting as a political activist, not to address and problematize this distinction would amount to intellectual cowardice. I know that comparing Russia with a hypothetical "West" will always yield more questions than answers, and I guess that's why, even though I would've loved to, I didn't get into the distinction in my last letter (which I had to jot down quickly while at my sewing machine). I'd never have time to say as much as I was thinking, sitting here in jail in one of those Special Economic Zones, the zones of institutionalized exploitation.

But recent political events have left me completely enraged: the appalling trial of Alexei Navalny and the Bolotnaya Square demonstrators,[1] which has degraded all of Russia; the introduction of language into the Constitution of the Russian Federation limiting free speech; laws that protect the "faithful" from offense, while codifying inequalities between those of "traditional" and "non-traditional" sexual

---

1   In late 2011, Moscow's Bolotnaya Square became the epicenter of vocal anti-corruption protests. Among the leaders was Alexei Navalny, a Russian lawyer, blogger, and activist. A consistent critic of Putin's government, Navalny has been arrested repeatedly. In July 2013 (the month this letter was written) he was sentenced to five years' forced labor on charges of fraud and embezzlement; the following day he was released from custody. Later that year, he came in second in Moscow's mayoral elections.

orientation. I have to speak out about my country's political and economic practices. The last time I was so infuriated was October 2011, when Putin announced his third term. The rage, indignation, and steely determination I was feeling then led to the creation of Pussy Riot. What will such feelings lead to this time? Time will tell.

I hope thinking through the specifics of Russia's situation might be of some use to you.

Who knows—it might be productive to consider the practices of a country where those who decide the fates of people, ideas, creative energies, and entrepreneurial and political initiatives consult not a meticulous, considered portrait of the situation, as in Europe, but rather a post-expressionist spasm of color. By contemplating the state that holds me in this labor camp, you might just answer your own perplexing questions about the creation of a stable, ethico-political feeling that can unite winds of discontent. If we want to understand the future of global capitalism, we need to consider its past. In the Russia of today, of Putin's third term, a vintage politics is masquerading as new—global capitalism reenacting its past before our eyes.

How exactly is this going to be useful?

Again, I insist that even the most developed capitalist formulation presupposes hierarchization, normalization, and exceptions. You quote Marx saying that "constant revolutionizing of production [and] uninterrupted disturbance of all social conditions ... distinguish the bourgeois epoch from all earlier ones." Agreed, we see upheavals in all social relations, but they don't cancel out exploitation and standardization. Instead, the outsourcing you often criticize comes into play. Antiquated techniques of discipline migrate to the Third World, into countries like mine, rich in raw materials. Of course, in the so-called "developed" world, disciplinary power doesn't disappear—but there are more bases of production and they're spread farther apart, so that the implementation of disciplinary power can be softer, more yielding in the face of resistance. Meanwhile, "developing" countries have cornered the market in discipline, which develops a horrific, archaic character. (For a striking example, consider the law "On Offenses Against the Emotions of the Faithful"—the comeuppance on such "offenses" is a three-year deprivation of actual, personal liberty, which in Russian penal practice always includes forced labor.)

And here in Russia, I'm keenly aware of the cynicism with which "developed" countries regard "developing" ones. The "developed" ones exhibit a conformist loyalty to governments that manhandle and suppress their citizens—a little rich for my taste. The US and Europe are glad to collaborate with a Russia where medieval laws have become the norm and the jails swell with prisoners of conscience. They're glad to collaborate with China, where things are happening that would make your hair stand on end. So the question arises: what are the acceptable limits of tolerance? When does it cease to be tolerance and become instead collaborationism, conformism, even criminal complicity?

The most common justification for this kind of cynicism goes something like this: "It's their country, let them do what they want." But that's just not viable, since countries like Russia and China have been enfranchised as equal partners in the system of global capitalism (which, it turns out, is by no means anti-hierarchic and rhizomatic everywhere). Russia's resource-based economy, and the Putin regime that draws strength from it, would be completely undermined if the political principles being forfeited by the buyers of its petroleum and gas were rendered visible. Even so small a gesture as Europe's passage of its own Magnitsky Act[2] would be important in principle, its implications primarily moral. A boycott of the 2014 Sochi Olympics could likewise serve as an expression of ethics. Instead, the world's continuing collusion in Russia's resource-based economy shows implicit support for, even approbation of, the Russian regime (not in words, of course, but rather in the flow of capital). It demonstrates a desire to protect the global economy's status quo and division of labor, that is, the current economic and political hierarchy. This is ample cause for concluding that the scope of anti-hierarchic trends in contemporary capitalism has been significantly overstated by Western theorists.

You quote Marx saying "all that is solid melts into air." Here I sit, in a country where the ten people who run and

---

2   Sergei Magnitsky was a Russian accountant who, after alleging that government officials had overseen the plunder of state holdings, was arrested by Russia's Interior Ministry. Detained without charge for 358 days—a week short of the legal maximum—he died suspiciously in custody on November 16, 2009, having previously been beaten and telling doctors he feared for his life. Three years later, the US government implemented the Magnitsky Act, a law restricting the access of Russian officials complicit in the incident to the US and its banking system. Russia responded with a similar law barring entry into that country by officials complicit in US torture and indefinite detention programs.

profit from the most important spheres of the economy are quite simply Vladimir Putin's oldest friends—buddies from school, the people he plays sports with, cronies from his KGB days. What could be more elitist, more deadening than that? What else to call it except feudalism?

And then, Marx adds: "all that is holy is profaned." In a country where even a passing mention of religious images, ideas, and understandings might carry with it the threat of three years' hard labor, this characterization of the "bourgeois epoch" (made in 1840!) can't but elicit nervous laughter.

My idea's pretty simple: I think it would be helpful for Western theorists to set aside their colonial Eurocentrism and consider global capitalism in its entirety, encompassing all regional variants. Maybe then some of them will come around to my perspective that the "mad flux" of "late" capitalism is in fact one of the most successful and far-ranging maneuvers in the history of humanity. I'm in no way suggesting that anti-hierarchic trends don't exist. For that matter, far be it from me to essentialize all advertising as superficial, inauthentic, and insincere. But advertising does impose a structure on commodities, and is in this sense a part of the process of production. So while I'm not calling for the rejection of advertising as a "false mask," I am calling for us to remember that all advertising has something to keep silent about, something it must render absent. And public critical theorists, inasmuch as they're engaged in critique rather than PR for "late" capitalism, should be studying the workings of this silence, exposing it to the light of analysis (rather than unreflexively parroting as their own theories global capitalism's image of itself—this seems to me what we see happening in Hardt and Negri).

Very seductive, an idea like "hyper-dynamic deterritorialization." From time to time, I succumb to its charm. But I guess I've been saved from overindulging, and from the kind of depression Guattari suffered, by living in a country that over and over again confronts me with palpable evil, staggering in its enduring, deep-rooted corporeality. I think I know exactly "what body, what mind is going through transformation and becoming" (Berardi) as I serve my "deuce"[3] (Putin) in lockdown.

All my sincere thanks to you, Slavoj, for this correspondence; I impatiently await your reply.

Your Nadya

---

3   In an interview for a TV special celebrating his sixtieth birthday on October 7, 2012, Putin, asked about Pussy Riot, said that the court had "slapped them with a deuce," referring to the women's two-year sentence. He then added, "I have nothing to do with this. They asked for it, they got it."

"I would like to conclude with a provocation"

Slavoj to Nadya, December 12, 2013

Dear Nadya,

I think our conversation should go on, because we left it open at a crucial point. In your last message, you emphasized the importance of taking into account the diversity among different countries, and how this diversity demands different forms of struggle. I fully agree, of course, but I would just like to add that this very diversity has to be located within the totality of global capitalism.

The Hegelian notion of totality to which I refer here is not an organic Whole, but a critical notion—to "locate a phenomenon in its totality" does not mean to see the hidden harmony of the Whole, but to include in a system all its distortions ("symptoms," antagonisms, inconsistencies) as its integral parts. In other words, the Hegelian totality is by definition "self-contradictory," antagonistic, inconsistent: the "Whole" which is the "True" (Hegel: "*das Ganze is das Wahre*") is the Whole *plus* its symptoms, the unintended consequences which betray its untruth. For Marx, the "totality" of capitalism includes crises as its integral moments; for Freud, the "totality" of a human subject includes pathological symptoms as indicators of what is "repressed" in the official image of the subject. The underlying premise is that *the Whole is never truly whole*: every notion of the Whole leaves something out, and the dialectical effort is precisely the effort to include this excess, to account for it. Symptoms are never just secondary failures or distortions of a basically sound System—they are indicators that there is something "rotten" (antagonistic, inconsistent) at the very heart of the System. Or, to shift to a brutally concrete case: if you want to talk about global capitalism, you have to include Congo, a country in disarray, with thousands of drugged child-warriors, but as such fully integrated into the global system. And the same holds for Russia.

We should always bear in mind that global capitalism does not automatically compel all its subjects into a hedonist/permissive individualism. The fact that, in countries which have recently undergone rapid capitalist modernization (like India), many individuals stick to their so-called traditional (premodern) beliefs and ethics (family values, rejection of unbridled hedonism, strong ethnic identification, preference for community ties over individual achievement, respect for elders, etc.) in no way proves that they are not fully "modern," as if only those in the liberal West can afford direct and full capitalist modernization, while those from less developed Asian, Latin American, and African countries can only survive the onslaught of capitalist dynamics with the help of traditional values, i.e., as if such values are only needed when local populations are not able to survive liberal capitalism by adopting its own hedonist-individualist ethics. Post-colonial "subaltern" theorists who see the violent modernity of global capitalism as disruptive of traditional ties are here thoroughly wrong: on the contrary, fidelity to premodern ("Asian") values is paradoxically *the very feature that allows countries like Singapore or India to follow the path of capitalist dynamics even more radically than Western liberal countries*. Appeals to traditional values enable individuals to justify their ruthless engagement in market competition in ethical terms ("I am really doing it to help my parents, to earn enough money so that my children and cousins will be able to study..."). We can say something similar about today's China: it is wrong to claim that China faces the choice of either becoming a truly capitalist country or of maintaining a Communist system which inevitably thwarts full capitalist development. This choice is a fake one: in today's China, capitalist growth is exploding not in spite of Communist rule but because of it—far from being an obstacle to capitalist development, Communist rule guarantees the optimal conditions for an unbridled capitalism.

In short, global capitalism is a complex process which affects different countries in different ways, and what unites the protests in their multifariousness is that they are all reactions against different facets of capitalist globalization. The general tendency of contemporary capitalism is towards further expansion of the reign of the market, combined with progressive enclosures of public space, sweeping cuts in public services, and a rising authoritarianism in the functioning of political power. It is in this context that the Greeks protest against the reign of international financial capital and their own corrupt and inefficient clientelist state increasingly unable to provide basic social services; that Turks protest against religious authoritarianism and the commercialization of public space; that Egyptians protested against a corrupt authoritarian regime supported by the Western powers; that Iranians protested against a corrupt and inefficient religious fundamentalist rule, etc. What unites these protests is that they all deal with a specific combination of (at least) two issues: a more or less radical economic one (from corruption and inefficiency to outright anti-capitalism) and a politico-ideological one (from demands for democracy to demands for overcoming the standard multiparty democracy). And does the same not hold for the Occupy Wall Street movement? Beneath the profusion of (often confused) statements, Occupy Wall Street incorporated two basic insights: 1) a discontent with capitalism *as a system*—the problem is the capitalist system as such, not any particular corruption; and 2) an awareness that the institutionalized form of multi-party democracy is incapable of holding back the excesses of capitalism, i.e., that democracy has to be reinvented.

There are, of course, many traps awaiting those engaged in these struggles. Let me take the case of Turkey. The motto that united those who protested in Taksim Square was "Dignity!"—a good but ambiguous slogan. The term is appropriate insofar as it makes it clear that protests are not just about particular material demands, but about the protesters' freedom and emancipation. In the case of the Taksim Square protests, the call for dignity not only referred to corruption but was also, and crucially, directed against the patronizing ideology of the Turkish prime minister. The direct target of the Gezi Park protests was neither neoliberal capitalism nor Islamism, but the personality of Erdoğan: the demand was for *him* to step down. Why? What made him so annoying as to become the target of both secular educated protesters as well as of anti-capitalist Muslim youth, the object of a hatred which fused them together? Here is how my friend Bülent Somay explains it:

> Everybody wanted PM Erdoğan to resign. Because, many activists explained both during and after the Resistance, he was constantly meddling with their lifestyles, telling women to have at least three children, telling them not to have C-sections, not to have abortions, telling people not to drink, not to smoke, not to hold hands in public, to be obedient and religious. He was constantly telling them what was best for them ("shop and pray"). This was probably the best indication of the neo-liberal ("shop") soft-Islamic ("pray") character of the JDP rule: PM Erdoğan's utopia for Istanbul (and we should remember that he was the Mayor of Istanbul for four years) was a huge shopping mall and a huge mosque in Taksim Square and Gezi Park. He had become "Daddy Knows Best" in all avenues of life, and tried to do this in a clumsy patronizing disguise, which was quickly discarded during the Gezi events to reveal the profoundly authoritarian character behind the image.

Is "shop and pray" not a perfect late-capitalist version of the old Christian *ora et labora*, with the worker or toiling peasant replaced by the consumer? The underlying wager is, of course, that praying (fidelity to the old communal traditions) will make us even better "shoppers," i.e., participants in the global capitalist market. However, the call for dignity is not only a protest against such patronizing injunctions; dignity is also the appearance of dignity, and in this case the demand for dignity means that I want to be duped and controlled in such a way that proper appearances are maintained, that I don't lose face—is this not a key feature of our democracies? This is how our democracies function—with our consent: we act *as if* we are free and freely deciding, silently not only accepting but even *demanding* that an invisible injunction (inscribed into the very form of free speech) tells us what to do and think. As Marx recognized long ago, the secret is in the form itself. In this sense, in a democracy, every ordinary citizen is effectively a king—but a king in a constitutional democracy, a king whose decisions are only formal, whose function is to sign measures proposed by the executive administration. This is why the problem of democratic rituals is homologous to the big problem of constitutional democracy: how to protect the dignity of the king? How to maintain the appearance that the king effectively decides, when we all know this is not true? What we call a "crisis of democracy" occurs not when people stop believing in their own power, but, on the contrary, when they stop trusting the elites, those who are supposed to know for them and provide the guidelines, when they realize, with some anxiety, that "the (true) throne is empty," that the decision *really is* now theirs. There is thus in "free elections" always a minimal aspect of politeness: those in power politely pretend that they do not really hold power, and ask us to freely decide if we want to give it to them—in a way which mirrors the logic of a gesture meant to be refused.

So, back to Turkey, is it only this type of dignity that the protesters want, tired as they are of the crude and blatant ways in which they are cheated and manipulated? Is their demand merely: "We want to be duped in the proper way— at least make an honest effort to cheat us without insulting our intelligence!" or is it really something more? If we aim at more, then we should acknowledge that the first step of liberation is to dismiss the appearance of false freedom and openly proclaim our un-freedom. The first step towards women's liberation, for example, is to reject the appearance of respect for women and openly proclaim that women are oppressed—today's master more than ever does not want to appear as the master.

Does this mean that we should simply get rid of the masters? Here, I would like to conclude with a provocation. A true Master is not an agent of discipline and prohibition, his/her message is not "You cannot!" or "You have to…!", but a releasing "You can!"—what? Do the impossible, i.e., what appears impossible within the coordinates of the existing constellation—and today, this means something very precise: you can think beyond capitalism and liberal democracy as the ultimate framework of our lives. A Master is a vanishing mediator who gives you back to yourself, who delivers you to the abyss of your freedom: when we listen to a true leader, we discover what we want (or, rather, what we always already wanted without knowing it). A Master is needed because we cannot accede to our freedom directly—to gain this access we have to be pushed from outside, since our "natural state" is one of inert hedonism, of what Alain Badiou calls the "human animal." The underlying paradox here is that the more we live as "free individuals with no Master," the more we are effectively non-free, caught within the existing frame of possibilities—we have to be compelled or disturbed into freedom by a Master.

There was a trace of this authentic Master's call even in Obama's slogan from his first presidential campaign: "Yes, we can!" A new possibility was thereby opened up. But, one might object, did not Hitler also do something formally similar? Was his message to the German people not "Yes, we can…"—kill the Jews, crush democracy, attack other nations? A closer analysis immediately brings out the difference: far from being an authentic Master, Hitler was a populist demagogue who carefully played upon people's obscure desires. It may seem that in doing so he followed Steve Jobs' infamous motto: "A lot of times, people don't know what they want until you show it to them." However, in spite of all there is to criticize about Jobs, in his own understanding of the motto he was close to being an authentic Master. When asked how much research Apple undertakes into what its customers want, he snapped back: "None. It's not the customers' job to know what they want … we figure out what we want." (In India, thousands of impoverished intellectual workers are employed in what are ironically called "like-farms," where they are miserably paid to spend the whole day in front of a computer screen endlessly clicking "like" buttons on pages requesting visitors to "like" or "dislike" a specific product. In this way, a product can be made to appear very popular and so seduce ignorant prospective customers into buying it, or at least checking it out, following the logic of "there must be something in it if so many customers are so satisfied!"—so much for the reliability of customer reactions...) Note the surprising turn of this argumentation: after denying that customers know what they want, Jobs doesn't go on with the expected reversal—"it is therefore our task (the task of creative capitalists) to figure out what they want and 'show it to them' on the market." Instead, he says: "we figure out what *we* want." This is how a true Master works: he doesn't try to guess what people want; he simply obeys his own desire and leaves it up to others to decide if they want to follow him. In other words, his power stems from his fidelity to his desire, from refusing to compromise on it. Therein lies the difference between a true Master and, say, the Stalinist leader who pretends to know (better than the people themselves) what people really want (what is really good for them), and is then ready to enforce it on them even against their will.

Just as I was finishing this letter, I learned that Nelson Mandela died—was he an authentic master? In the last two decades of his life, Mandela was celebrated as a model of how to liberate a country from the colonial yoke without succumbing to the temptation of dictatorial power and anti-capitalist posturing. In short, Mandela was not Mugabe, and South Africa remained a multi-party democracy with a free press and a vibrant economy well integrated into the global market and immune to hasty socialist experiments. Now, with his death, his stature as a saintly wise man seems confirmed for eternity: there are Hollywood movies about him; rock stars, religious leaders, sportsmen and politicians from Bill Clinton to Fidel Castro are all united in his beatification.

Is this, however, the whole story? Two key facts are obfuscated in this celebratory vision. In South Africa today, the miserable life of the poor majority remains broadly the same as it was under apartheid, and the rise of political and civil rights is counterbalanced by growing insecurity, violence, and crime. The main change is that the old white ruling class has been joined by a new black elite. Secondly, people remember the old African National Congress which promised not only the end of apartheid, but also more social justice, even a kind of socialism. This much more radical ANC past is gradually being obliterated from memory. No wonder that anger is growing among the black poor.

South Africa is here just one version of the recurrent story of the contemporary Left. A leader or party is elected with universal enthusiasm, promising a "new world"—then, sooner or later, it stumbles upon the key dilemma: should one dare to interfere with the capitalist mechanisms, or should one decide to "play the game"? If one chooses to disturb the mechanisms, one is very swiftly "punished" with market perturbations, economic chaos, and the rest. This is why it is all too simple to criticize Mandela for abandoning the socialist perspective after the end of apartheid: did he really have a choice? Was the move towards socialism ever a real option?

It is easy to ridicule Ayn Rand, but there is a grain of truth in the famous "hymn to money" from her *Atlas Shrugged*: "Until and unless you discover that money is the root of all good, you ask for your own destruction. When money ceases to become the means by which men deal with one another, then men become the tools of other men. Blood, whips and guns or dollars. Take your choice—there is no other." Did Marx not say something similar in his well-known formula about how, in the universe of commodities, "relations between people assume the guise of relations among things"? In the market economy, relations between people can appear as relations of mutually recognized freedom and equality: domination is no longer directly enacted or visible as such. What is problematic is Rand's underlying premise: that the only choice is that between direct or indirect relations of domination and exploitation, with any alternative dismissed as utopian. However, we should nonetheless bear in mind the moment of truth in Rand's otherwise ridiculously ideological claim: the great lesson of state-socialism was effectively that a direct abolishment of private property and market exchange, in the absence of concrete forms of social regulation of the process of production, necessarily resuscitates direct relations of servitude and domination. If we merely abolish the market (and so market exploitation) without replacing it with a proper form of the Communist organization of production and exchange, domination will return with a vengeance, and with it direct exploitation.

The general rule is that, when a revolt breaks out against an oppressive half-democratic regime, as was the case in the Middle East in 2011, it is easy to mobilize large numbers of people with slogans that can only be described as "crowd pleasers"—for democracy, against corruption, etc. But then we gradually approach more difficult choices: when the revolt succeeds in its immediate goal, we come to realize that what really bothered us (social corruption, our un-freedom, humiliation, lack of prospects for a decent life) continues in a new guise. The ruling class here mobilizes its entire arsenal to prevent us from reaching this radical conclusion. We are now told that democratic freedom brings with it its own responsibility, that it comes at a price, that we are not yet mature if we expect too much from democracy. In this way, they blame us for our failure: in a free society, so we are told, we are all capitalists investing in our own lives; it's up to us to put more time and effort into our education than into having fun if we want to succeed, etc.

At a more directly political level, US foreign policy pursued a determined strategy of damage control by way of re-channeling popular uprisings into acceptable parlia-mentary-capitalist constraints—as was done successfully in South Africa after the fall of apartheid regime, in the Philippines after the fall of Marcos, and in Indonesia after the fall of Suharto, etc. It is at this precise conjuncture that radical emancipatory politics faces its greatest challenge: how to push things further after the first enthusiastic stage is over, how to take the next step without succumbing to the catastrophe of the "totalitarian" temptation—in short, how to go further than Mandela without becoming Mugabe.

If we want to remain faithful to Mandela's legacy, we should thus dispense with the celebratory crocodile tears and focus on the unfulfilled promises his leadership gave rise to. We can also safely surmise that, on account of his undoubted moral and political greatness, he was at the end of his life aware of how his very political triumph and elevation into a universal hero was itself the mask of a bitter defeat. His universal glory is but a sign that he didn't really disturb the global order of power—which certainly cannot be said of Pussy Riot.

Awaiting your answer, and with the hope that the two of you who are still in prison will soon be released,

Slavoj

"When you put on a mask, you leave your own time"

Nadya to Slavoj, March 11, 2014

Dear Slavoj, a good day to you,

As fate would have it, your last letter found me already out of prison. Which came as quite a surprise, since my time there was marked by a completely unfounded, irrational certainty that prison goes on forever.

But in some sense, prison really does go on forever. My "co-conspirator" Masha Alyokhina and I lost no time after our release in founding the "Zona Prava"[1] movement, the goal of which is the reeducation of prison wardens and

---

1 Often translated "Justice Zone," the phrase in fact means something closer to "Zone of Right." The Russian word, like the English word "right," denotes simultaneously "right" as an axiomatic political entitlement, "right" as opposed to left spatially and politlcally, and "right" meaning "correct." "Zone" is also Russian criminal slang for "jail."

the establishment of a protest training program inside the camps. We're beginning with women's camps, since female prisoners are the ones most totally deprived of voice. Why is this so? Probably because women have long had inculcated into them a deep a sense of weakness, of their need for a big, strong man… Our work is already turning up evidence that a lot of them buy into this garbage. And their "big, strong man," since these women are prisoners, can come only from the prison administration. Our task, Zona Prava's task, is to provide them an equally big and strong alternative.

In due time, we and Zona Prava will have to answer an old question: can the—pardon me—subaltern speak? How can sister-inmates develop their own language, existing alongside the official one spoken by prison administrators? How can they draw up the map to another world, a world different than that of the administrators? The story of the subject's development in prison is extremely meaningful.

A Russian jail is an island of institutional totalitarianism, a site where thought and action become unified. Further, the template for this unification has little in common with other officially promulgated prisons, like our conception of motherhood, orthodox religion, and respect for the law. In fact, so long as the administration isn't inconvenienced, a person's decline and fall is encouraged. A high level of aggression is encouraged, and a foundation is set for baseless anger and hatred. By what right can we call this a system of "corrections"? Is it not, rather, the rubric for a slavishly obedient, oppressed, and humiliated existence? Or an existence that is two-faced, cynical, and hypocritical, one that survives by the reptilian law of "you die today, I'll wait until tomorrow"? What can we make of people being expected to form their personalities in a place where they can barely even try rethinking the assumptions that form their daily lives? How is such a personal reformation possible when every act of protest is met with diabolical evil and reprisals from the agents of state authority?

Prison goes on forever. And because it's run not by official rules but according to its own internal processes, it makes you understand how the structures of power, subordination, and protest are related in a community whose ultimate purpose is unification and degradation. In a community for whose creation any elite of unbounded power de facto strives.

The only thing we can offer up in opposition to the current transformation of our communities into a prison is an absurd, unfounded faith that another state of affairs is possible. Will we be able to infect others with our dreams before we find ourselves again deprived of voice—returned, perhaps, to prison?

◆

The other day we traveled to Nizhny Novgorod's Penal Colony No. 2, where Masha had been held. We went to lend our support to some female inmates who'd had the temerity to disagree with the infallible prison administration. These women took the camp administration to court, challenging the legality of their humiliatingly meager pay of $7–$10. At the Nizhny Novgorod train station, we were attacked by a gang who doused our eyes with a caustic liquid. We put up no physical resistance, but only asked our attackers to explain why they were doing this. We were left with chemical burns to our eyes. Masha suffered a concussion and needed stitches.

Facing physical violence was a test of my usually friendly and composed response to opposition. To what degree can this goodwill be preserved? At what point does such a situation become an actual threat to one's life? When I reflect how I might conduct myself, I take comfort in the story of how St. Paul, fleeing his pursuers, had himself lowered from the Damascus city walls in a basket, "In Damascus the governor under Aretas the king kept the city of the Damascenes with a garrison, desirous to apprehend me: And through a window in a basket was I let down by the wall, and escaped his hands." (2 Cor 11:32–33) This episode has for me become key, opening as it does the possibility of resistance, of saving one's own life, of being calculating, even sly, in apostolic Christianity.

◆

Slavoj, it wasn't too long ago that you suggested it might be a good idea for Masha and me to speak our minds about Edward Snowden. This is no simple thing to do when Snowden is living in your country under the protection of the same intelligence services that have ordered and overseen physical violence against you and your friends. At the same moment that we two were in prison, Edward Snowden was finding himself in quite an awkward situation—a fighter for the free dissemination of information, he found himself in Russia, where, like it or not, his presence inevitably conferred legitimacy on the Kremlin's information policy. The same Kremlin that was directing an aggressive propaganda campaign on TV, destroying all independent channels, condoning the murder of independent journalists—professionals, heroes like Anna Politkovskaya. Snowden, however, had been cornered into a dismal position from which he could not expose any of this. He now lives in Russia, but he can't tell the truth about how information is collected and disseminated here. He has no choice but to keep his mouth shut. Russia's intelligence and propaganda sectors have used Snowden for their own grubby games. And for me, as one of Russia's activists, it's horrible to watch. There's no doubt that his persecution is a drastic misstep by the US, which is keeping far too busy destroying the possibilities for true democracy around the world. This error is made visible by Russia's cynical use of the whistleblower to stabilize the Kremlin's own reactionary information policy.

◆

Once in an interview you said that you wanted to write an essay criticizing Pussy Riot for our inordinate conservatism. I think I know what you were getting at, but it would be inordinately interesting all the same for this essay to see the light of day.

Pussy Riot is a mask: a simplifying, modernizing mask. Prison, confinement, these are also masks, different masks, ones that help people of our generation to shake off cynicism and irony. When you put on a mask, you leave your own time, you abandon the world in which any sincerity will be mocked, you move into the world of cartoon heroes, where Sailor Moon and Spiderman, those consummate modern role models, can be found. Somewhere in that world our other role models live on, too: Kazimir Malevich, Dziga Vertov, Wassily Kandinsky.

Pussy Riot has proved so effective that its promise—simple to the point of impossibility, minimalist to the point of indecency—rings loud and clear. The masks that members of Pussy Riot wear hold, if any, a therapeutic function: yes, we belong to a generation raised on irony, but we also put on masks to reduce that impotent irony. We go out in the streets and speak plainly, without varnish, about the things that matter most.

◆

The most penetrating speeches, writings, and actions are born of modernist condensation, of the modern age. True crises—imprisonment, war, the crisis of democracy that you have described in which people grow alarmed, stop trusting the elites, and realize that it is now *truly* up to them alone—catalyze the emergence of such historic periods.

No one is speaking out more truthfully about contemporary Russia than the May 6th protesters,[2] now sentenced to the camps for as many of four years' deprivation of liberty. Their final words in the courtroom are worth remembering: "We've been taken hostage by the authorities. We've been tried for the sore feelings bureaucrats still harbor for the civil disobedience of 2011 and 2012, for the apparitions that still haunt the police bosses. They're forcing us on stage in their

2   Tolokonnikova here is referring to the Bolotnaya case, the prosecution of participants in a protest on May 6, 2012, the evening before Putin's inauguration for his third term as president

theatrics of societal punishment." (Alexei Polikhovich) "I know that even in prison I'll be freer than most because my conscience will be clear." (Alexandra Dukhanina) There are few today speaking such simple, clear, passionate truths—all of them behind bars.

In Russia, recent days have seen a sincere discussion of the threat of armed conflict in Crimea. Journalists, poets, and artists are composing incendiary texts against war. Schoolteachers are extending alarmed exhortations to everyone they know to join the peace demonstrations. People have poured into the streets with placards bearing anti-war slogans, even releasing doves, though we all know that in a minute everyone's going to be manhandled and arrested by the cops. I, for one, welcome this mood, which is trading out doubt and irony for a new, decisive voice.

By the way, the modernist and zealous declarations of today are being used far more successfully by Russia's officially sanctioned journalism establishment than by the independent or opposition media. The mouthpieces of state propaganda, I'm forced to admit, have learned a lot from the early Soviet avant-garde's methods of agitation. Sharing Pierre Bourdieu's slogan "Pour un savoir engagé," I would like to see more combustion and personal, emotional involvement in the statements and gestures of those who today rise up against unfreedom, social corruption, humiliation, and lack of prospects for a decent life in Russia.

It is impossible not to sympathize with the passionarity[3]

---

3 "Passionarity" (*passionarnost'*) is a concept developed by the heterodox Soviet ethnographer Lev Gumilev, son of the major poets Nikolai Gumilev and Anna Akhmatova. It refers to the will of an

of the Ukrainians involved in Euromaidan. The persever-
ance, the courage, and—sure, I'll say it—the heroism with
which Ukrainians, from the lowliest workers to the upper
echelons of management, have defended their political inter-
ests comprise, without question, an utter miracle. As surely
a miracle as the turning of water to wine for the Marriage
at Cana.

I respectfully await your reply,

Nadya

---

ethnos to expand in population, influence, and geographic territory,
which arcs over the duration of a people's existence.

"A new and much more risky heroism will be needed"

Slavoj to Nadya, March 18, 2014

Dear Nadya,

Let me first express my joy—I am glad that you are now free, and even more glad that your struggle goes on. You have, of course, my full solidarity with Zona Prava. I also fully support Pussy Riot's style of performance. What you wrote about masks reminds me of what Nietzsche wrote apropos *Hamlet*: "what must a person have suffered if he needs to be a clown that badly!" One should unconditionally defend the apparently irreverent and clownish attitude of Pussy Riot's actions as the only appropriate reaction to traumatic and violent events—let me make an extreme example to clarify this point. A Bosnian cultural analyst was surprised to discover that among those people whose relatives died in Srebrenica, dozens of jokes about the Serb massacre circulated. Here is one of them, which refers to the way of buying beef in old Yugoslavia when usually the butcher would ask,

"With or without bones?" The joke goes: "I want to buy some land to build a house close to Srebrenica. Do you know what the prices are?" "Prices vary, depending on what kind of land you want—with or without bones." Far from expressing tasteless disrespect, such jokes are the only way to deal with the unbearably traumatic reality: they render quite adequately our helpless perplexity, belying pathetic compassion with victims of atrocities as itself a truly tasteless blasphemy.

Let me address the rumor you mention that I intend to write an essay criticizing Pussy Riot for their inordinate conservatism. Frankly, I don't know where this rumor originated—it is simply not true, and furthermore "conservative" is to me not necessarily a critical notion. From Marx on, the truly radical Left was never simply "progressist"— it was always obsessed by the question, what is the price of progress? Marx was fascinated by capitalism, by the unheard-of productivity it unleashed. He just insisted that this very success engenders antagonisms. And we should consider the same in the context of today's progress of global capitalism, to keep in view the dark underside that is fomenting revolts. What this implies is that today's conservatives are not really conservative: fully endorsing continuous capitalist self-revolutionizing, they just want to make the system more efficient by supplementing it with some traditional institutions (religion, etc.) to contain its destructive consequences for social life and to maintain social cohesion. A true conservative today is the one who fully admits the antagonisms and deadlocks of global capitalisms, the one who rejects simple narratives of progressism, and is attentive to the dark obverse of progress. In this sense, only a radical Leftist can be today a true conservative.

I did, however, make a remark about solidarity with Snowden, about the danger of becoming engulfed by the liberal human rights movement, and on this I have more to add. First, let me emphasize that I totally agree with your characterization of Snowden, the compromises he had to make, and the way he can be (and is) exploited by Putin. My only point is, what other choice did he have? He is exploited and manipulated in the same way (and much more so, undoubtedly) that human rights liberals try to manipulate Pussy Riot. This is why I think that it would be very important for Snowden, Assange, Manning, etc., to make it clear that they cannot be reduced to simple anti-Americanism. Snowden should be defended not only because his acts annoyed and embarrassed the US secret services. What he revealed is something that not only the US but also all other great and not-so-great powers, from China to Russia and Germany to Israel, are doing to the extent they are technologically able to do so. His acts thus provided a factual foundation to our earlier premonitions of how much we are all monitored and controlled—the lesson is a global one, it reaches far beyond the standard US bashing. We didn't really learn from Snowden or from Manning anything we didn't already presume to be true, but it is one thing to know it in general and another to have concrete data. It is a little bit like knowing that one's sexual partner is playing around—one can accept the abstract knowledge of it, but pain arises when one learns the steamy details, when one sees the photographs. Sometimes, we learn such steamy details from smaller marginal countries that pass security measures in a much more open and direct way. In the summer of 2012, the Hungarian parliament passed a new national security law that

> enables the inner circle of the government to spy on people who hold important public offices. Under this law, many government officials must "consent" to being observed in the most intrusive way (phones tapped, homes bugged, email read) for up to two full months each year, except that they won't know which 60 days they are under surveillance. Perhaps they will imagine they are under surveillance all of the time. Perhaps that is the point. More than 20 years after Hungary left the world captured in George Orwell's novel *1984*, the surveillance state is back ... Now, if the Fidesz government of Prime Minister Viktor Orbán finds something it doesn't like—and there's no legal limit to what it may find objectionable—those under surveillance can be fired. The people at the very top of the government are largely exempt from surveillance—but this law hits their deputies, staffers and the whole of the security services, some judges, prosecutors, diplomats, and military officers, as well as a number of "independent" offices that Orbán's administration is not supposed to control.[1]

And here is how the Hungarian government justifies such measures:

---

1 Kim Lane Scheppele, "*1984*, Hungarian Edition," http:// krugman.blogs.nytimes.com/2013/06/17/1984-hungarian-edition/

Officials of the Hungarian government will say that what they are doing is nothing novel. Other countries, they will point out, have ways to determine whether high-level officials have played fast and loose with state secrets or whether people holding the public trust are corrupt. The US government has now been shown to be gathering up everyone's phone calls and emails, so how can anyone be critical of what the Hungarian government is doing?[2]

When confronted with such facts, should not every decent US citizen feel like a baboon suddenly overwhelmed by the shame of its protruding red butt? Assange, Manning, and Snowden are exemplary cases of the new ethics that befit our era of digital control and communications. They are no longer just whistle-blowers who denounce illegal practices of private companies (banks, tobacco and oil companies) to the public authorities; they denounce these public authorities themselves when they engage in the "private use of reason." We need more Mannings and Snowdens in China, in Russia, everywhere. States like China and Russia are of course much more oppressive than the US—just imagine what would have happened to someone like Manning in a Russian or Chinese court: in all probability there would be no public trial, a Chinese Manning would just disappear! However, one should not exaggerate the softness of the US tactics, though true they doesn't treat prisoners as brutally as China or Russia. Because of the global technological priority of the US, they simply do not need to take an openly

---

2 Ibid.

brutal approach, though they are more than ready to apply it when necessary. In this sense, the US are even more dangerous than China insofar as their measures of control are not perceived as such. That is to say, in a country like China, the limitations of freedom are clear to everyone, there are no illusions about it, the state is an openly oppressive mechanism, whereas in the US, formal freedoms are mostly guaranteed so that most individuals experience their lives as free and are not even aware of the extent to which they are controlled by state mechanisms. Such whistle-blowers do something much more important than state the obvious by denouncing openly oppressive regimes, that is, rendering public our already directly experienced unfreedom: instead they render public the unfreedom that underlies the very situation in which we experience ourselves as free.

This feature is not limited to the control of digital space: it pervades thoroughly the form of subjectivity that characterizes the "permissive" liberal society. Since free choice is elevated to a supreme value, social control and domination can no longer appear to infringe on a subject's freedom: it has to appear as, and be sustained by, the very self-experience of individuals as free. There are a multitude of forms in which unfreedom appears in the guise of its opposite: when we are deprived of universal healthcare, we are told that we have been given a new freedom of choice, to choose our healthcare provider; when we can no longer rely on a long-term employment and are compelled to search for new precarious work every few years, we are told that we have been given the opportunity to re-invent ourselves and discover unexpected creative potentials that lurk in our personalities; when we are obliged to pay for the education of our children, we are told that we become "entrepreneurs of the self," as if we should be acting like a capitalist who chooses freely how he will invest the resources he possesses (or has borrowed) into education, health, travel... Constantly bombarded by such imposed "free choices," forced to make decisions for which we are not even properly qualified or sufficiently informed, we more and more experience our freedom as a burden that causes unbearable anxiety. Unable to break out of this vicious cycle as isolated individuals, since the more we act freely the more we are enslaved by the system, we need to be "awakened" from this "dogmatic slumber" of fake freedom from outside, by the push of a Master figure.

This brings me back to my central point: it is absolutely crucial to insist on the universality of our struggle. The moment we forget that Pussy Riot and WikiLeaks are moments of the same global struggle, everything is lost, we have sold our soul to the devil. And I think that we must maintain the same attitude towards the events in Ukraine. I, again, totally agree with you that the the protests that toppled Yanukovich and his gang were a miracle comparable to the Arab Spring. They were triggered by the Ukrainian government's decision to prioritize good relations with Russia over the integration of Ukraine into the European Union. Predictably, many anti-imperialist Leftists reacted to the news about the massive protests with their usual racist patronizing of the poor Ukrainians: how deluded they are, still idealizing Europe, not seeing that Europe is in decline and that joining the European Union would just make Ukraine an economic colony of Western Europe sooner or later, pushed into the position of Greece. What these Leftists ignore is that Ukrainians were far from blind about the reality of the European Union, but fully aware of its troubles and disparities. Their message was simply that their own situation is much worse. Europe's problems are still a rich man's problems—remember that in spite of the terrible predicament of Greece, African refugees are still arriving there en masse, drawing the ire of Rightist patriots.

Second, and much more important, what does the "Europe" the Ukrainian protesters refer to stand for? It cannot be reduced to a single idea: it spans from nationalist and even Fascist elements up to the idea of what Etienne Balibar calls *égaliberté*, freedom-in-equality, the unique contribution of Europe to the global political imaginary, even if it is today ever more betrayed by European institutions and people themselves. And between these two poles is the naïve trust in European liberal-democratic capitalism. What Europe should see in Ukrainian protests is its best and its worst, and to see this clearly, Europe has to look outside itself onto a Ukrainian scene.

Rightist nationalism, although relatively marginal in general, should not be underestimated. One of the signs of the deep shift in ideological hegemony that Western Europe has undergone in the last decade is the request of the new Right to establish a more balanced view of the two "extremisms," the Rightist one and the Leftist one: that is, to treat the extreme Left in the same way Europe after WWII treated the extreme Right. Although Communist critics of Stalinism were naïve and full of their own flawed ideas, long before Solzhenytsin "the crucial questions about the Gulag were being asked by Left oppositionists, from Boris Souvarine to Victor Serge to C.L.R. James, in real time and at great peril. Those courageous and prescient heretics have been somewhat written out of history (they expected far worse than that, and often received it)."[3] This large-scale critical movement was inherent to the Communist movement, in clear contrast to Fascism: "nobody can be bothered to argue much about whether fascism might have turned out better, given more propitious circumstances. And there were no dissidents in the Nazi Party, risking their lives on the proposition that the Fuehrer had betrayed the true essence of National Socialism."[4] Precisely because of this immanent tension at the very heart of the Communist movement, the most dangerous place to be in the time of the terrible 1930s purges in the Soviet Union was at the top of the *nomenklatura*: in a couple of years, 80 percent of the Central Committee and Red Army Headquarters members were shot. Furthermore, one should also not underestimate the "totalitarian" potential, as well as direct outright brutality, of the White counter-revolutionary forces during the Civil War: had a White victory been the case,

the common word for fascism would have been a Russian one, not an Italian one. *The Protocols of the Elders of Zion* was brought to the West by the White emigration ... Major General William Graves, who commanded the American Expeditionary Force during the 1918 invasion of Siberia

---

3 Christopher Hitchens, *Arguably*, New York: Twelve, 2011, p. 634.

4 Ibid., p. 635.

(an event thoroughly airbrushed from all American text-
books), wrote in his memoirs about the pervasive, lethal
anti-Semitism that dominated the Russian right wing and
added, "I doubt if history will show any country in the
world during the last fifty years where murder could be
committed so safely, and with less danger of punishment,
than in Siberia during the reign of Kolchak."[5]

As if echoing this dark past, Putin's official Russia
presented the Crimean referendum as a choice against
(Ukrainian) Fascism, while the entire European neo-Fascist
Right (Hungary, France, Italy, Serbia) was firmly supporting
Russia. (And another irony: Ukrainians were tearing down
statues of Lenin, forgetting that the golden era of Ukraine
was in the first decade of the Soviet Union when they established their full national identity.) But Putin's Russia is not
an exception here: from the Balkans to Scandinavia, from
the US to Israel, from central Africa to India, a new Dark
Age is looming, with ethnic and religious passions exploding, and the Enlightenment values receding. These passions
were lurking in the shadows all the time, but what is new
now is the outright shamelessness of their display. So what
are we to do in such a situation? Mainstream liberals are
telling us that, when basic democratic values are under threat
by ethnic or religious fundamentalists, we should all unite
behind the liberal-democratic agenda of cultural tolerance,
to save what can be saved and put aside dreams of a more
radical social transformation. However, the conflict between

5   Ibid.

liberal permissiveness and fundamentalism is ultimately a *false* conflict—a vicious cycle of the two poles generating and presupposing each other.

So what about the liberal-democratic capitalist European dream? One cannot be sure what awaits Ukraine within the EU, beginning with austerity measures. In my books I often use the well-known joke from the last decade of the Soviet Union about Rabinovitch, a Jew who wants to emigrate. The bureaucrat at the emigration office asks him why, and Rabinovitch answers, "There are two reasons why. The first is that I'm afraid that in the Soviet Union the Communists will lose power, and the new power will put all the blame for the Communist crimes on us, the Jews and there will again be anti-Jewish pogroms—" "But," interrupts the bureaucrat, "this is pure nonsense, nothing can change in the Soviet Union, the power of the Communists will last forever!" "Well," responds Rabinovitch calmly, "that's my second reason." We can easily imagine a similar exchange between a critical Ukrainian and a European Union financial administrator. The Ukrainian complains, "There are two reasons we are in a panic here. First, we are afraid that the EU will simply abandon us to Russian pressure and let our economy collapse—" The EU administrator interrupts him, "But you can trust us, we will not abandon you, we will tightly control you and advise you on what to do!" "Well," responds the Ukrainian calmly, "that's our second reason."

So yes, the Euromaidan protesters were heroes, but the true fight begins now, the fight for what the new Ukraine will be, and this fight will be much tougher than the fight against Putin's intervention. A new and much more risky heroism will be needed here. The model of this heroism is found in the Russians that you mentioned, Nadya, who courageously oppose the nationalist passion of their own country and denounce it as a tool of those in power. What is needed today is to make the "crazy" gesture of *rejecting the very terms of the conflict* and proclaiming the basic *solidarity* of Ukrainians and Russians. One should begin by organizing events of fraternization across the imposed divisions, establishing shared organizational networks between the authentic emancipatory core of Ukrainian political agents and the Russian opposition to Putin's regime. This may sound utopian, but it is only such crazy acts that can confer on the protests a true emancipatory dimension. Otherwise, we will get just the conflict of nationalist passions manipulated by oligarchs who lurk in the background.

But let me now really conclude on a more personal note. After reading your last letter, I found myself by chance listening to "Stenka Razin," that most universally known of Russian folk songs, and its content reminded me of your point about how crucial it is for the subaltern to speak for themselves, and to break out of the situation where the sympathetic others (humanitarians, etc.) speak for them. The song describes how the mighty Cossack ataman was proudly sailing on the Volga with his beautiful young bride, a kidnapped Persian princess, at his side. But then, from behind, he heard a murmur: "He has exchanged us for a woman! He spent only one night with her, and in the morning he has become a woman himself!" The furious Stenka immediately decided what to do:

"I will give you all you ask for
Head and heart and life and hand."
And his voice rolls out like thunder
Out across the distant land.

And she, with downcast eyes,
more dead than alive,
silently listens to the drunken
words of the ataman:

"Volga, Volga, Mother Volga
Wide and deep beneath the sun,
You had never such a present
From a Cossack of the Don.

So that peace may reign forever
In this band so free and brave
Volga, Volga, Mother Volga
Make this lovely girl a grave."

Now, with one swift mighty motion
He has raised his bride on high
And has cast her where the waters
Of the Volga roll and sigh.

Now a silence like the grave
Sinks to all who stand and see
And the battle-hardened Cossacks
Sink to weep on bended knee.

> "Dance, you fools, and let's be merry
> What is this that's in your eyes?
> Let us thunder out a chantey
> To the place where beauty lies."

For me, the crucial moment of the song is the final reversal: when the common warriors get what they demanded from Stenka, their reaction is stupefaction, horror, even weeping, and Stenka, in the true gesture of a Master, makes them accept the gift of what they wanted as a source of joy—you asked for it, now you got it, so be merry! But the feature that is really shocking for us today is the absence of the woman's point of view: she was first kidnapped, raped, then killed, so how did she experience the situation? What about her own song, rendering her own horror? I think that you, Nadya, and your fellow fighters are creating something similar to the imagined song of the Persian princess…

So I am looking forward to our common struggle, with friendship and solidarity,

Slavoj